Edward John Phelps

Lectures on Topics Connected with Medical Jurisprudence

Delivered before the Medical Department of the University of Vermont

Edward John Phelps

Lectures on Topics Connected with Medical Jurisprudence
Delivered before the Medical Department of the University of Vermont

ISBN/EAN: 9783337764128

Printed in Europe, USA, Canada, Australia, Japan

Cover: Foto ©Paul-Georg Meister /pixelio.de

More available books at **www.hansebooks.com**

LECTURES

ON TOPICS CONNECTED

WITH

MEDICAL JURISPRUDENCE

DELIVERED BEFORE THE

MEDICAL DEPARTMENT

OF THE

UNIVERSITY OF VERMONT

BY

E. J. PHELPS.

APRIL, 1881.

Reported Stenographically by Sumner Gleason and Chas. H. Nichols,
and printed for the use of the Medical Class.

BURLINGTON :
THE FREE PRESS ASSOCIATION.
1881.

LECTURE I.

MEDICAL EVIDENCE.

–

Medical jurisprudence, gentlemen, is that combination of legal and medical science sometimes found necessary to the administration of justice. Its learning is principally medical, its application altogether judicial. When taught by the physician to the lawyer, it treats of medicine; when the lawyer instructs the physician, it treats of law. It is wholly from the legal side that I shall attempt to deal with the subject, in the few lectures I shall be able to offer you. I could not supplement your medical instruction; certainly I shall not try. And even of the law that belongs to the subject, much is only useful to the lawyer, and but a part is ever actually serviceable to the physician. I shall therefore confine myself to some of those practical considerations and suggestions, which, as it seems to me, may be valuable to you in your coming professional life; troubling you with no theories, with no speculation, with none of the theoretical philosophy, if it may be dignified by that title, which attaches to this subject as to so many others, endless in its extent, and very rarely useful in its results.

The sole connection, with a single exception, you will ever be likely to have professionally—as physicians—with the department of medical jurisprudence, is in the capacity of medical witnesses. The one exception, if strictly it may be called so, is the liability of a physician, civilly and criminally, for his own professional conduct. On that point I shall have something to say before the course is completed. But with that exception, the whole subject, from the legal standpoint, so far as you are practically concerned, narrows itself down to a consideration of the rights, the privileges, the duties, the responsibilities, and the requirements of the medical witness. What I have to say might therefore have been more properly entitled, observations upon medical evidence, rather than upon medical jurisprudence.

Now in the first place what is "expert testimony?" And what, especially, is meant by the term "medical expert?" Ordinary testimony in a court of law, is confined to the statement of those facts which a man learns by the use of his physical senses. He may state what he has seen, what he has heard (from the proper quarter), what he has tasted, or smelt, or physically felt; and that is all. The operations of his mental consciousness are entirely excluded. His opinions, inferences, conclusions, expectations, theories, hopes, fears, and thoughts, are all shut out. When he has stated the facts he personally knows, the inference, the conclusion, the opinion to be formed upon them, must be formed by the court or jury, that has the case to decide. So that an ordinary witness, no matter how humble his capacity, requires no previous preparation. The very idea of preparation usually suggests that he is expected to tell something besides the truth. He has but one rule to observe, and that is to tell the truth, as far as he knows it, in the simplest way. But the administration of the law further demands, and therefore allows, the class of testimony I have mentioned, called "expert testimony;" that is to say, the testimony of men who by their familiarity through study or special experience, or both, with a science, an art, or sometimes an industry, are permitted to state not merely facts, but opinions, scientific truth in the abstract, theories, conclusions, and their application to particular cases. Who is a competent expert in any given case, is a question that is decided by the court. Upon a preliminary inquiry to the witness selected and called by a party to the cause, as to his experience and acquaintance with the subject, the court determines whether or not he is a competent witness for that purpose, whose testimony may be heard for what it may be worth.

Experts are of two kinds, practical and scientific. Practical experts are those who have acquired a peculiar skill in some unscientific specialty, by actual experience in it,—as the mechanic, or sometimes the farmer, in respect to certain branches of their callings. That is an humble class of expert testimony, not usually of great importance. It is not commonly dignified with the name of expert testimony, although strictly speaking it is such. The more important class, and that to which your attention is required, is that of scientific experts; those who have become sufficiently acquainted with the principles of some established science like medicine, surgery, chemistry, engineering, or mechanics. On such subjects, those accomplished or learned in them are received as expert witnesses, and are called scientific experts, or, within your own profession, medical experts, or medical witnesses.

Now, as a medical witness, you are permitted and will often be required to state, in the first place, abstract scientific truth in your own department ; such as the anatomy of man ; the structure of the body : the various organs, and their functions; the pathology of disease, its source, its progress, its diagnosis, its prognosis, its treatment, its consequences, the origin of life, the cause of death. Then you will be called on further, to give opinions in respect to particular cases of injury, disease, or death. "What is the matter with this man? What was the cause of it? What should be the treatment? Is he likely to recover?" In short, the whole range of material inquiries, that may arise in respect to any given case. And those questions may be put under three different conditions. 1. You may be asked to testify in respect to some case that you have personally examined, either because you have attended it in a medical capacity, or have been called to examine it for the purpose of forming an opinion as a witness, to be stated in court. 2. You may be required to answer the same questions, upon conditions and symptoms detailed by some other physician, in respect to a case you have never seen : and where the inquiry assumes such statement to be true. 3. And finally, you may be subjected to the same questions, upon supposed or theoretical cases. These latter inquiries may be put, not only where the case supposed is taken to be or claimed to be the real case in dispute, but also for the purpose of testing the capacity of the witness, his knowledge, his intelligence, his fairness. Of course there is a limit to that sort of inquiry, which rests largely in the discretion of the court, and depends somewhat upon the witness to whom such questions are addressed. In these three ways, therefore, you may be called upon to give opinions, conclusions and theories, sometimes in the abstract, and sometimes in respect to individual cases. That constitutes the testimony of the medical expert.

While every man in the community can be compelled to attend court as a witness in any case in which either party thinks proper to summon him, whether he knows anything about the case or not : and although a physician or a surgeon like any other man may be brought into court as a witness, and compelled to attend there in response to a subpœna, and to state all material facts within his personal knowledge, he is not obliged to testify to opinions, or to give what I have attempted to define to you as expert testimony. A physician has a right, if he pleases, in response to inquiries of that sort, to decline to express opinions. He must judge for himself whether he has sufficient acquaintance with the subject— whether he possesses an opinion that he is willing to swear to. And one of the values of that privilege to the medical profession is, that it enables them to command a compensation for attending as expert witnesses, beyond the small fee that the law pro vides for ordinary witnesses. It is customary, and it is proper, that physicians who are called into court to testify to scientific truths or opinions, and perhaps to examine cases to qualify themselves to testify in regard to them, should receive an adequate compensation for their services. Of course cases arise in courts of justice as in private practice, where charity or humanity call for the gratuitous services of the physician as an expert witness, as they call for his services at the bed-side. But there is no legal obligation on the part of the medical witness, to give his opinion as an expert.

Communications made to physicians by the parties on whom they are attending, are not protected by law from dis closure in courts, if the physician should happen to be called as a witness, except in a few states where special statutes on the subject exist. In my judgment they ought everywhere to be protected, and the confidential communications between a patient and his physician should be placed on the same footing with similar communications between a client and his counsel or attorney, which cannot be disclosed. I hope, ultimately, such will everywhere be the law. But as the general law now stands, you may be in most states compelled in courts of justice to disclose communications and statements of your patients that were confidential in their character, and which perhaps it may be very important to the patient should remain confidential. And that being the case, only two suggestions can be made on the subject. One is that physicians should be careful, where they perceive that what is said to them may be the topic of judicial inquiry, or may expose the patient to some legal consequences, neither to invite nor receive confidence beyond what their professional duty makes necessary. The other suggestion is, that it is comparatively rare that witnesses are called upon in courts to testify upon a point, on which their knowledge has not been previously ascertained. You will not be very likely, therefore, to be asked for such a disclosure, unless it has in some way trans-

pired that you are able to make it. And I need not say that
in respect to communications of that sort from patients,
very great care should be taken by the physician, that no one
becomes aware that the enterprise of interrogating him on the
stand concerning them, would be likely to be successful. In
short, they never should be disclosed at all, so long as it can
be avoided without perjury, or a direct violation of the order
of the court.

Let me say one thing further on the general topic of
medical and surgical evidence. Your profession has an exclusive monopoly of it. There is no other witness who under
any circumstances will be heard in a court of justice on that
subject. The whole matter is absolutely in your hands. And
though you are not called upon as judges to decide the cause,
you furnish all the materials on which the questions turn which
do decide the cause, where it depends upon medical evidence.
It is the only monopoly you have ;—not the only monopoly, in
my judgment, you ought to have: but in most of the states of
our country a man may be doctored by a quack or an impostor if he pleases, and it is the pernicious right of the quack or
the impostor to doctor him. The medical profession have
generally no legal monopoly of the practice of medicine or
surgery. But the equally important function of supplying
the courts in all cases where it becomes necessary, with all the
medical truth, and all the opinions in respect to individual
cases, on which they must proceed, belongs exclusively to the
physician.

Now, I ask you, young men, with your professional life
before you, to pause on the threshold of the subject, and try
to appreciate adequately the importance of this great duty.
And you will see upon a very little reflection, that there is
no duty you are likely to be confronted with in your professional capacity, more important than that of supplying to the
tribunals of your country, the evidence upon which questions of
this sort are to be determined. If I were to venture to pass

any criticism upon a profession so honored and so honorable as yours, deduced, as all that I have to say to you will be, from a long experience in courts, where I have seen many physicians brought forward as witnesses—I say if I were to venture upon any criticism, it would be, that it is too often the case that physicians come forward as witnesses, without reflecting upon, without realizing, the very great importance that may be attached to what they say. It is important in the first place to the parties concerned. Life is often involved in it. There is hardly a day in the year, but somewhere within the range of the common law, some life is trembling in the balance, dependent upon medical testimony. Thousands of men have gone to their death upon such evidence, and as many more have been saved from death by it. It involves character and liberty very often, which are better than life. It involves family and social relations; it comes between husband and wife, parent and child, brother and sister. And it involves constantly, large amounts of property, great public interests, and all sorts of private concerns. It is important likewise to the administration of justice, that most precious of all public functions, too often, like good health, unappreciated till impaired; and especially important, because such evidence, unlike ordinary testimony, can rarely be answered or refuted outside of the profession from which it comes. In respect to unscientific subjects, a reckless or mistaken witness can usually be contradicted. The knowledge and experience of courts and juries themselves, on such topics, enable them to estimate evidence at its true value, and to perceive its mistakes. But when they enter the field of scientific learning, and its application to particular controversies, they must go by the light they receive. The most enlightened magistrate, the most intelligent jury, are unable to judge over the heads of the profession. If physicians disagree, the triers must settle the dispute as well as they can ; but it is the preponderance of the medical evidence after all, when ascertained, that must determine the issue.

2

It may be doubted, distrusted, suspected, but there is no other resource.

And it is further to be kept in mind, that the importance of such evidence extends not less to its manner than to its substance. It is extremely liable to be misunderstood by un scientific minds, unless expressed with clearness, accuracy and completeness. It is easily perverted where room for perversion is left. Here more than elsewhere is it true, that

" Many a shaft at random sent,
Finds aim the archer never meant."

Bear in mind, then, always, in approaching this subject, that the law of the land places in your hands a great trust, which as all trusts do, carries with it a corresponding obligation, and a corresponding responsibility. It trusts the profession to which you belong ; it trusts the training you have received ; it trusts the moral character which true intellectual training always ought to develop. And it leaves with confidence the whole duty in your hands.

Now, alive, as I hope you will always be, to the serious importance of the errand you are upon, whenever you cross the threshold of a court of justice for this purpose, allow me to offer you some suggestions on the subject of the character, the manner, and the proprieties of that sort of evidence. And do not regard me, I pray you, as undervaluing either the sub ject or yourselves when I say, as the first thing to be kept in mind, that a physician should not permit himself to be made an expert witness, which as I have already shown you requires his own consent, nor assume to occupy that responsible posi tion in any case, until he is very sure that he has an adequate knowledge of the topic in hand. The range of medical testimony is as large as the theory and practice of medicine itself. There is no case you can be called to, from the teething of the infant to the most insidious disease that ever baffled the skill of a physician, or the most critical and difficult operation that surgical science ever achieved, but may become the sub ject of medical testimony. Of course there are many topics which gentlemen in the profession have no right to be ignorant of. If they are, they have no right in the profession. On this ordinary range of topics, every regularly educated physician should be and is at home always. But there are many others, of less frequent occurrence, that may come under the review of judicial proceedings, on which a physician may have some general, perhaps vague and inadequate knowledge, but no thorough acquaintance. He has never made them the sub ject of particular study. In the course of his practice he has never or rarely encountered them. They are out of the every day routine of medical life. On such subjects, a partially in formed physician ought to decline to take the responsible situation of an expert witness. It is no discredit to a man to say, "I do not know." That is often a creditable answer, and it is remarkable how often it is a true one. A man need therefore be neither afraid nor ashamed to leave expert testi mony on rare and out-of-the-way points, to those with whom they have been a study or a specialty. This seems all very ob- vious when it is stated ; it is pretty much the same as saying, "Do not testify to what you do not know." But I have some times seen professional gentlemen—not often, I am happy to say—make their appearance on the witness stand, to testify glibly as experts upon subjects with which they were very im- perfectly acquainted. And I have seen them go away with a lively and realizing sense of the sifting process that superfi- cial knowledge, that worst kind of ignorance, undergoes in a court of justice.

Again, while I never knew a man succeed in conveying to others knowledge that he did not possess, I have known many who have entirely failed in trying to convey the knowl- edge they did undoubtedly possess. A man may be full of information which he cannot express. He has not, it is said, the gift of language. But the difficulty in expressing himself is usually much less the want of language, than the want of

that clearness of idea that comes from systematic, calm, and
continuous thought. Knowledge not digested by reflection,
is just as valueless as food that is undigested in the stomach.
The curse of our time is the vast quantity of undigested
knowledge that is everywhere prevalent. Thousands of force-
pumps are at work in all directions forcing knowledge into
people. It is wonderful how much men know.—and it is won
derful, often, how little good it does them.

I might hold up before you a crystal, symmetrical, translu
cent, beautiful, and in the other hand a handful of mud. The
one you treasure; the other you throw out at the window.
Yet chemistry might inform you, that in that handful of mud
were all the constituents of the crystal. The difference is that
they have not been separated, and they have not been crystal
lized. That silent mysterious process in the laboratory of na
ture, which has formed the crystal somewhere and somehow,
has not acted upon these crude materials. There is the same
difference, as it seems to me, between the mental processes of
the man who has knowledge that has been crystallized into clear,
distinct, accurate perceptions, and those of the man who is
crammed full of knowledge that he has never digested. He
who is too lazy to think, as many are, or too busy to think, as
many more are, had better keep his mouth shut, because he
never will distinguish himself by anything he is likely to
say. The application of these suggestions that I desire to
make, is this: When you are going to appear in a court of
justice as an expert, to attempt to throw light upon any sub
ject, it is not enough, though indispensable, that you possess
an adequate knowledge of it; you must first subject your
knowledge to that careful reflection, that shapes it into definite,
clear, intelligible, unmistakable propositions. Then the necessary language will follow. You need take no thought what
you shall speak; you need consult no rhetoric to teach you
words. Clear and accurate thought is the parent of that clear

and accurate expression, which the way-faring man can understand as well as the professor.

A very great lawyer, now dead, Judge Curtis of Boston told me that in his younger days he once had the advantage of being called into consultation with Mr. Webster, in respect to an important cause. And as he had considered it very carefully beforehand, he stated to Mr. Webster, what he conceived to be the leading proposition of law on which the case was likely to turn. Mr. Webster thought of it a moment, and said, " Let us write it down." He drew up to the table, took his pen, and carefully wrote out the proposition, not in many words, and then considered it for a while with attention. "That will do," said he, " that will stand. Always write your proposition down, Brother Curtis, always write it down." He wrote only the proposition : he did not write out what was to be said in support of it : and he did so in order to put it beyond mistake, that the idea in his mind was not a vague, indeterminate idea that would perish in the stating, but one that could stand looking in the face. It is a maxim that may be well commended to all professions, to write down the cardinal points : those on which the question turns. Then you are sure that what you think you see clearly in the mind's eye, you do see clearly, can reflect upon clearly, and can express clearly, when the occasion comes.

I shall continue this subject to-morrow.

LECTURE II.

MEDICAL EVIDENCE.

(Continued.)

Perhaps, gentlemen, a part of what I said yesterday, may be thought more applicable to a public speaker than to a med ical witness. But testifying on scientific subjects is a sort of public speaking, and requires the best qualifications that belong to that art. In the lecture we had the pleasure of hearing afterwards from Dr. Garland, you had an admirable specimen of the clearness of diction I had tried in my imperfect way to describe; and I do not know that I can add anything more or better on the subject than to say, that such is the sort of talk courts like to hear from medical witnesses; but, I am sorry to say, do not hear as often as they could wish. An accomplished medical witness is as rare as a highly accomplished surgeon. I have listened sometimes with as great admiration as I ever felt at any display of public speech, to the elucidation of scientific subjects by medical witnesses; to which even the great words of the Genesis of the earth might almost without profanation be applied, "Let there be light, and there was light." On the other hand, I have seen excellent physicians on the witness stand, with no idea at all except that of doing their duty, placed in a false position, misunderstood, attacked, ridiculed, their evidence perverted, and, perhaps, used in the end to establish some conclusion which they would have entirely repudiated ; and largely, though not altogether, as I shall try to point out in what I have to say to-day, owing to a want of that very clearness, accuracy, and certainty of diction and of expression, which, as I have tried to show, cannot be artificially acquired, and comes from only one source in the world.

Assuming, then, that the medical witness approaches a court of justice with an adequate sense of the importance of the business he is upon ; with a competent knowledge of the subject he is to testify about : and with that clearness of understanding, born of reflection, which will enable him to give lucid expression to what he means to say, there are some further requisites to successful medical testimony, to which I shall invite your attention. I ask you to remember, and, if necessary, to write down, four cardinal rules, founded, as I had occasion to say yesterday, not upon any views of my own, but upon an experience which all judges and lawyers will corroborate. And the first is, not to permit yourself under any circumstances, to be enlisted in a cause, in sympathy, feeling or fact, on one side or on the other. This rule is the most important of all, and it is the most difficult of all. It is a hard thing for any one to witness a contest, without feeling a sympathy or an interest. A man of vigorous intellect is liable to a sort of joy of battle :—*gaudet certamine.* Then you are brought into the cause by one side ; you are the plaintiff's witness or the defendant's witness : you are very naturally consulted and perhaps employed by your friends ; you participate to some extent in their deliberations ; you believe the side on which you are called is right, and that the theory or the scientific fact you testify to is right : you may see or think you see, likewise, a conflicting theory, set up perhaps by medical experts on the other side, which you believe is wrong, and which you believe is going to result in injustice. Now it is no imputation upon a man when he sees his friend involved, or indeed anybody involved in a contest where he supposes him to be right, and where his own testimony is opposed and in danger of being overthrown by what he considers to be wrong, that he should have a feeling on the subject, and that the feeling should insensibly show itself. But it is this very feeling that requires to be suppressed in the witness, who goes on to the stand to present under oath the material for deciding difficult questions, and on whom the responsibility for the truth is altogeth er cast. He goes into court, not as the advocate, charged with the interests of one side, but as the judge goes, bound to deal impartially with both sides. I hope to see the day when the selection of medical experts will be made by the court and not by the parties: so that such witnesses will be brought in, not on one side or the other, but rather like an arbitrator or a referee, chosen for both sides, and equally the representative of both. But as the law is, and always has been, the party who desires to use the testimony of a medical expert, selects and examines him.

There are two sufficient reasons why at any effort, and as I have said, it costs an effort, this bias should be avoided. The first is, that it will invariably color the testimony given. It is not in the power of the human mind that it should be otherwise. You may swear to a statement, but you can never safely swear to an argument. The moment you charge your self with the presentation of one side of a question, your presentation becomes an argument: and the very essence of an argument is, that it is upon one side. There may be an im partial presentation of both sides, but when you begin to sus tain your own opinion against an adversary, you enter upon an argument: and such testimony will be inevitably colored. A little color sometimes goes a great way in a tribunal not competent to criticize statements of that kind, or to weigh them as a physician would, and insensibly the statement be comes stronger than it should be.

Another sufficient reason against bias in the witness, is that whether the testimony is actually influenced or not, the

impression will get into the jury-box that he is enlisted on
one side. He appears to be the plaintiff's or the defendant's
man, trying to support his own theory, and to put down that
of the other side. He is not impartial. He is saying what he
would not say if he did not feel an interest in the contest.
That, of course, detracts very much from the force of the evi
dence ; it puts the physician in a position he would be very
sorry to be placed in, if he was aware of it, and defeats the
object for which he is called. On the other hand, when a
man is able to go before a court, and with clearness, precision and certainty, state the scientific facts and truth it re
quires, without apparent bias, without fear of one side or
favor of the other, his words carry weight—and deserve
weight.—And there is no more gratifying position for a scien
tific witness to occupy, than when he is able to command in
an important cause the confidence of both sides, so that what
comes from him will be received as the unbiased and uncolored
truth. Remember that you are not charged with the conduct
of the cause. It is not for you to see that justice takes place,
or that injustice does not take place, except so far as your
own evidence is concerned. The court and the counsel are
charged with that. You have only to discharge your duty,
and to leave the responsibility of trying the cause where it be
longs, and where it will certainly fall in the end.

The second rule to which I ask your attention, is this :
In your anxiety to avoid the appearance of partiality, do not
go to the other extreme, and become indefinite and uncertain.
I have heard witnesses testify, who were so sensitive on the
point I have been discussing, and so afraid of appearing to be
on one side, that nothing definite could be got out of them.
Whatever you make up your mind to say, make it definite and
clear. There is no question in the world that does not admit
of a definite answer. If a man were to ask me the cause of
the Aurora Borealis, for example, I could give him a prompt,

definite and decided answer. I should say "I do not know."
This rule has a special application to medical testimony, be
cause so many questions that arise, and are put, do not admit
of a decided or certain solution. Such are questions as to fu
ture results, that cannot be foretold with certainty. But if
you understand the subject, you can convey an intelligible
idea of what you think the chances are, and what they depend
upon, so that the hearer, who learns from you that the result
is uncertain and cannot be demonstrated, will form an intelli
gent judgment of how uncertain it is, what are the chances,
and what are the conditions to be regarded in estimating them.
And so with other questions, such as those touching the char
acter of disease, or the cause of death. Many of them do not
admit of a positive answer, or a demonstration that you can
swear to, but do admit, however, of a definite and clear treat
ment, that will give the hearer all there is to be given on the
subject.

This brings me to the third suggestion I desire to make,
and that is : Do not employ in a court of law (or anywhere
else except before educated physicians), the technical phraseol
ogy that belongs to the medical profession. It is the only ac
curate phraseology, I admit. Its propriety and necessity are
undoubted ; but do not use that sort of language where it can
not be understood. If you assume at all to try to make a
point clear to laymen, not educated in medicine or surgery,
furnish yourself with language that is not derived from the
Greek. Technical terms are a constant and fertile source of
ridicule among those who do not comprehend them. The witness is placed in an unjust position, and the force of his testi
mony is lost.

This morning I took out of the postoffice a circular of a
legal stenographer, containing some specimens of his work as a
reporter. He has given extracts on this slip of paper from the
language of various speakers, and among others a medical ex-

pert. who testified in a cause in another State. It illustrates so well what I am trying to say, that I read it :

"Ecchymosis occurs without any injury from a certain condition of the blood globules or the blood itself, particularly of the blood globules, being in a condition of debility and weakness themselves, consequent upon debility and weakness of the blood vessels themselves, to such a degree that stagna tion occurs ideopathically, and disintegration of the blood takes place, and the coloring matter of the blood globules, or hematin, is dissolved in the fluids, and the blood by endosmose passes out in the areolar tissues."

The ordinary mind might be surprised to learn, that this evidence was designed to throw light upon the black and blue spots on a man who had been knocked over by. a chair. Doubtless that gentleman expressed with technical accuracy what he meant to convey. The difficulty was, that he put it into phraseology which conveyed no idea at all to the triers, and which was almost certain to expose him to ridicule.

And now while I have the reporter's paper before me, let me go back a moment to the subject of clearness of diction, and as I have read something at the expense of the medical profession, let me read at the expense of my own, a specimen of the style of speech highly desirable to be avoided. A learned counsel, according to the reporter, once delivered himself as follows:

"I take 4.86 feet, the highest measurement they have given us, as the height of the floor above mean low tide, and then the width of the beams, 3x10 inches--the cross-joists, as they all told about—and the centre timbers, 12 inches square—taking all the testimony together, 12 inches for the beams—although they did not all know about that—yet there was room enough to allow a man to crawl under—8 or 10 inches—but I am content to call it 6 inches—and I contend nobody would allow less that—and adding 2 inches for the double floor—about 2 inches, I suppose, as they usually use inch boards—which would make 20 inches—but I am content to take it at one foot and a half, so as to be sure I am right—taking these highest measurements and the lowest estimate given by any gentleman, what will be the level of the ground compared with the city base or mean low water."

If I were to announce to you that a demurrer to the
rebutter puts in issue the sufficiency of the sur-rejoinder, I
should probably fail to convey any very useful or accurate
idea : and yet I have in those words stated with entire pre
cision a legal proposition, as a lawyer would state it, and in
the language lawyers and judges would understand. But you
would feel that you had a right to require, if it was necessary
that you who are not lawyers should understand the point,
that if I possessed a clear idea of it myself, and was not too
anxious to display my technical knowledge, I should furnish
myself with language that would enable you to comprehend it.
And so when you go into a court of law, to enunciate those
propositions belonging to your science, it is your duty and
your necessity to turn the subject over in your mind, until
you can make it understood by those to whom medical tech
nology is unknown ; until you are able to make the fracture
of a bone, the dislocation of a joint, and the surgical remedy
to be applied, as clear to the common mind, as you would the
fracture and repair of the axle of a wagon. You can do it if
you try. I know it can be done, because I have seen it done
with such excellent success.

There is one more rule I desire to impress, and that is, to
bear in mind that clause of the oath always administered to
witnesses, which requires them to tell, not only the truth, but
the whole truth. See to it that you go far enough in your
testimony to be fairly, as well as distinctly understood. Such
is your right. Although you are required to answer the questions which are put to you, when you have finished your an
swers the court will always allow you to add any further ex
planations you may deem necessary. So that if you have
been inquired of in the sharp way that has precluded you
from saying all that ought to be said in the first place, the
time comes, before you leave the stand, when you have an op
portunity and a right to say it. The examination may some
times be ingeniously devised, and inquiries artfully put,

with the view of drawing out just so much and no more of the physician's knowledge. Some things which the witness will state are wanted; other things which he will state, if he has a chance, are not wanted. It may be desired, for instance, to prove that a man had a certain disease which he did not have, and which the doctor will not swear he had.

"Doctor, did the man have such a symptom?"

"Yes."

"Does that symptom accompany this disease?"

"Yes."

"Did he have such another symptom?"

"He had."

"Is that symptom found in this disease?"

"It is."

"Did he have such a third symptom?"

"Yes."

"Does that belong to this disease?"

"Yes, it does."

"Now, doctor, when you find a patient with all these symptoms, does not it lead you to suspect the presence of this disease, and does not that subject immediately engage your attention?"

"Yes."

The examination terminates, the doctor comes off the stand, and after the trial says to the opposing counsel, "Why did not you ask me if the man had a certain other symptom which was the decisive one, and which he did not have? The symptoms named always accompany that disease, it is true, but they are likewise seen in other diseases; there is one symptom which is decisive; and the absence of that proves that he did not have the disease." "Why, then, did you not say so?" "Oh, I was waiting to be asked." Two excellent reasons may have existed for not asking the question. The counsel may not have known enough of medicine to know that it ought to be asked; or if he did, he feared to ask it of an adverse witness, with whom he had not conversed, and where he knew not what the answer might be. For all he knows, the question may have been inadvertently omitted on the other side, and the answer would be more damaging than all the doctor had said before. So the evidence is used, and perhaps successfully, as establishing the probability of the existence of the disease, or at least a reasonable doubt whether it did not exist.

While, as I have said, the medical expert is not charged with the conduct of the cause, in any way, he is charged with the duty of testifying, if he testifies at all, fairly enough, and fully enough, so that his testimony shall not be misunderstood, and above all that it shall not be so perverted, as to be used before a jury to establish the very fact he knows is not true.

Now, gentlemen, it is not given to many of us to be great: it is not given to many physicians to be great. It is enough for most of us, if we can be useful and respectable in our place and according to our measure, and discharge with fidelity those duties, perhaps modest and humble duties, we are brought face to face with in life. I have spoken of medical witnesses whom I have seen, men of great and rare power and felicity, in presenting to the mind, and especially to the un scientific mind, scientific truth. I should hardly hope that the profession generally could in this respect, more than in any other, be all brought up to its highest standard. But I undertake to say this: that any physician of respectable abil ity and respectable attainments, such attainments as are nec essary in order to graduate from an institution like ours, can come into a court of justice as a witness on a subject he un derstands, and which he has considered until his ideas are clarified, and if he will observe these rules I have tried to make plain, will always acquit himself creditably and usefully. He never will be the subject of successful ridicule; and not often of attempts at ridicule. His testimony will never be misunderstood, and he never will suffer the mortification and regret, of having in fact contributed to a result which was very far from his intention.

Much is often said about cross-examination : and people not familiar with courts think it a sort of rack or thumb-screw proceeding, that witnesses have a great deal to fear from. There is no intelligent child that needs to be afraid of any cross-examination he will encounter in the court room, if he tells the truth and the whole truth, in an unaffected way. You may possibly meet a blackguard at the bar—not many, I am happy to say—you may perhaps come across such a character, who would be glad to insult or brow-beat you, if he thought he could make anything out it. But he will generally be wise enough to know whether he is likely to make anything out of it or not. And a fair, impartial man, talking about what he clearly understands, taking no side, using simple phraseol ogy, careful to comprehend accurately what is asked of him, and then careful that his replies shall be definite and complete, has nothing whatever to fear from examination or cross-exam ination: especially if he adds to those qualifications, entire coolness and perfect courtesy, remembering always, that by his profession, if not otherwise, *he is a gentleman*, whatever those may be with whom he is brought in contact.

This brings me to the end of what I have to say on a subject, the importance of which, I repeat, is not sufficiently estimated by the profession upon which you are entering. Aside from its more general and public importance, it is im portant to the physician himself. It is a distinction, a great distinction, and, I may add, a lucrative distinction, as well as a very useful one, to become accomplished in the art of giving scientific testimony. Men of much calibre trouble themselves very little with the pursuit of reputation. The reputation that is good for anything is that which follows, not that which is run after. He who pursues with success the straightforward course of professional duty, may be surprised some day to find

himself the subject of a reputation he had neither sought nor
been conscious of. But those paths of duty, nevertheless,
which lead to the reputation that forms the basis of profes
sional prosperity, are not to be neglected or overlooked. And
I commend, even on this score alone, to your consideration,
the importance of becoming master hands in the discharge of
this special duty, which more or less all through your lives, and
more and more as you evince a capacity for it, and often in a
very conspicuous situation, you will be invited to perform.

LECTURE III.

INSANITY.

There are only a few out of the many topics, gentlemen, which might be usefully discussed in connection with the general subject of medical jurisprudence, to which I shall be able to ask your attention, in the brief course allotted to me. The subject of to-day's lecture is one of the most important of those topics—insanity. Of all the diseases and afflictions that beset humanity, and with which it is unhappily necessary for the physician to become familar, there is not one that is more subtle in its character, more diverse in its manifestations, more melancholy in its aspects, than that of mental derangement. The great poet has expressed in the most touching language, the appeal which those unfortunates often make to your profession, for a relief you can but rarely afford :

> "Canst thou not minister to a mind diseased ?
> Pluck from the memory the rooted sorrow,
> Raze out the written troubles of the brain,
> And with some sweet oblivious antidote,
> Cleanse the stuffed bosom of the perilous stuff
> That weighs upon the heart ?"

And when the inquirer finds his appeal in vain, he rejects altogether the art that fails in this supreme emergency :

> "Throw physic to the dogs,
> I'll none of it."

But it is only with the legal and judicial consequences of insanity that I have to deal—an important, but at the same time but a very partial branch of the subject : a subject that

4

in this age, when rest and quiet are apparently so fast becoming obsolete terms, and mental disorder is so greatly increasing, must more and more attract the attention and study both
of your profession, and of philanthropists.

The subject of insanity finds its way into courts of justice
in three connections. First, as a defence to criminal prose-
cutions; next, in its effect upon civil contracts; and third, as a
foundation for the judicial power of placing a person under
guardianship, and taking from him the control to which he
would be otherwise entitled, over his own property and his
own affairs. There is another subject in which insanity is
sometimes involved in judicial inquiry, and that is the power
to dispose of property by will; but I shall consider that
in another connection, and confine myself at present to
the three particulars I have stated. And the first and most
important in its public and its private application to judicial
proceedings, is the effect of insanity as creating an exemption
from criminal responsibility.

Insanity under our modern law—which is of comparatively
recent growth for the most part—is a defence against all criminal charges, where it exists in the degree which the law recognizes as sufficient. It applies to all offences, small as well
as great; a criminal motive being requisite always to make out
a crime; and the man who is incapable of motive, that is to say
incapable of rational motive, is consequently incapable of being
guilty of a criminal offence. One would suppose from what
he finds in the public press, that insanity was the special defence of the crime of murder, because we so rarely hear of it
in courts of justice in connection with any other charge. There
is no defence that, when it is well founded, appeals with more
force to humanity, as well as to justice, than that. It is not
only a legal defence, but it is one that excites the sympathy of
all who are capable of that emotion. On the other hand, there
is no defence that ever has been so much abused; until it has
come to be a scandal and a reproach in this country, above all

other countries where law prevails. Many a man is walking about to-day, as sane as we are, who has been acquitted of some foul assassination, on the score of an insanity that had its beginning, its end and its proof, in the crime it was held to justify—nothing ever heard of it before, nothing ever heard of it since. It is, I say, an infinite scandal and disgrace—the use that has been made of a defence, which, when true, is so mer itorious and so necessary: and I lay at the door of the medical profession, or a part of it, almost all the mischief that has ensued, and the injustice that has taken place, from the abuse of the defence of insanity. Not because all the evidence in cases of insanity, as in most other cases that involve scientific or medical questions, comes from your profession. I remarked the other day that you had a monopoly of the sources of evidence that were available to a court of justice on such subjects. But this disease is to some extent an exception, because it has such obvious manifestations, often not at all requiring a scientific or medical man to detect, that other evidence to prove it is admissible and useful, besides that of physicians. But I attribute the result I have spoken of to the physicians, because no doubtful case, probably, ever was tried involving that issue, in which the medical testimony was not substantially decisive one way or the other. So much is conceded to the better skill, the better judgment, and the closer power of observation of those trained as physicians, that their testimony on that subject has a controlling weight. No man could succeed for an hour in a court of justice upon the claim that he was insane, unless he could substantiate that claim by some respectable medical evidence. Of course I do not allude to cases of complete or general imbecility or mania, in which no serious question could arise. I am speaking of those cases in which the fact of insanity might fairly be the subject of dispute. The answer to such a claim by the triers would be conclusive. "If insanity exists, physicians can detect and measure it. Common humanity, if there were no other reason, would place the whole faculty at your disposal to furnish any evidence in such a case that is true. It is a duty no man would wish to avoid. Where, then, is the physician who has examined this case? Where is the expert in insanity that has tested it? If you can produce no such witness, you cannot expect to satisfy us." You see, therefore, the very great weight, the indispensable importance of medical testimony on the subject of insanity; and if the defence has been abused, if any man has been acquitted on that score, who ought not to have been acquitted, while opprobrium is cast upon the jury who found the verdict, and sometimes upon the judge who presided over the trial, and perhaps with more justice upon the counsel who set up a defence they ought to have known to be without foundation in truth, the real responsibility rests upon those men who come into court to state upon oath that impartial scientific truth, which they ought to be and generally are better judges of, than any one else.

Insanity is a term it is almost impossible to define with accuracy. What do you mean by saying that a man is insane? That is to say, how much must he be outside of a normal mental condition, to be called insane? If you set up a perfect mental standard, there are perhaps few of us that are not more or less insane. A perfectly sound mind would be as rare as an absolutely symmetrical body. What do you mean by saying a man is symmetrical, and free from physical deformity? Do you mean that he has the perfect symmetry of the Apollo Belvidere? That he has complete bodily perfection? What definition could you give to the term "sick"? When may a man be properly said to be sick? No physician can answer such a question, until you give him some criterion to go by. You must define what you mean by being "sick," before the physician could tell you whether the patient came up to that standard or not.

Insanity has been thus divided:

I. Congenital affection of the mind.

II. That which occurs from a subsequent cause, after the development of the mental faculties has once taken place.

Congenital insanity, or mental imbecility, which is the same thing, may be again divided into 1, total imbecility, as seen in persons commonly called idiots, and where there is substantially an absence of all or most of the mental faculties ; and 2, partial imbecility, a partial defect of the mental capacity, born with the subject. Then the class of mental derangement that occurs after sound faculties have once existed and have been developed, may be again divided into: 1. Mania, and 2. Dementia: the first signifying a derangement and disease of existing faculties; and the other signifying the absence of mental faculties in whole or in part, that is to say, the loss of faculties, that have once existed. It may be total or may be partial, and may be the result either of disease, of injury, or simply of old age. And mania, or the perversion or derangement of existing faculties, may be total, involving the whole organization of the mind, or it may be partial, limited in its effect, and often only monomania, that is, mania on one subject alone, in a man who is sane enough, to all appearance, upon all others. This division has seemed to me to cover the outlines of the subject of mental affection, as accurately as verbal definition can.

You will readily see, that as to several of these divisions no serious question can arise; and that they never could be the subject of judicial dispute. Idiocy, for instance, is plain enough in its manifestations. Of dementia, also, where a person has lost his mental faculties either in whole or in great part, the symptoms and the evidence are so plain and obvious, so different from those involved in the intricate and difficult task of tracing the mere perversion or derangement of faculties that are in themselves vigorous, that controversy in regard to it is not likely to arise. Dementia, then, like idiocy, may be

dismissed as a form of insanity not likely to occasion any
serious question or dispute; that is to say, after it has progressed far enough to have serious consequences. It is sometimes insidious in its beginning and in its earlier stages, but
rarely has a tendency to excite to crime even then. So mania,
where it is complete or general, where the patient is what would
ordinarily be called a maniac, or a lunatic; a man really desti
tute of mental motive, and acted upon by insane, uncontroll
able impulses, that cannot be assigned to any operation of the
mind; requiring to be confined, to keep him from destroying
his own life, or some other man's life or property; with no real
consciousness of what he is doing; not aware that he is killing
a man, or what he is killing him for;—that form of mania is
also too plain to be the subject of question. The two remain
ing branches of the classification I have given you, will there
fore comprehend all questions in respect to which medical
testimony is ever likely to be invoked in courts of law.
That is, cases of partial imbecility, where the defect is congen
ital, and yet where it is not so complete, so full, as to place
beyond doubt just how much there is of it and what it amounts
to; and cases of partial mania, resulting from disease, from
injury, from any cause adequate to produce it, and sometimes
applicable only to certain subjects, perhaps to a single subject.
Those are the cases in which the disputes arise.

Now, the field of speculation on this topic is unlimited
and inexhaustible. The psychological subtleties and the meta
physical theories connected with it are endless. The discussion of the question, what should and what should not be
regarded as insanity, has never terminated, and is likely to be
perpetual; and every man is quite at liberty to set up his own
standard, and to maintain it in his own way, and with as much
pertinacity as he pleases. But what you and I have to do
with the matter in its present connection, is simply to ascertain
the rule of law on the subject, and the true limits and manner
of its application; a rule that we did not establish, that we

could not change if we thought it wrong: and one which like most rules of the common law, will be found upon reflection to be right; so that it has a double claim to regard, not only as being the law, which should be enough, while it remains so, for all right-minded men, but likewise because it ought to be, and probably always will be, the law. When you have that criterion distinctly in mind, which you will perceive is as neces sary to be understood by the physician as by the lawyer, by the witness as by the advocate, you will be prepared to apply the proper test to any given case. To ask you, as I before said, whether a man is insane, is to ask a question that cannot be intelligibly answered, except in those plain cases that do not admit of dispute, until you are in possession of the cri terion, the test, the standard applicable to the case in hand. You will be called upon many times, probably, if you follow the practice of your profession, to examine men who are claimed to be, or thought to be, insane. Sometimes they may be so, and sometimes not. Sometimes there will be more or less foun_ dation for the claim, and yet after all no sufficient foundation: sometimes there is none at all: sometimes enough. The only guide is the rule of law: and rather than attempt to state that in my own words, I have taken the pains to transcribe from some of the many cases which might be produced, because this is a subject which has been widely discussed in many courts, two or three statements of the legal definition of such insanity, as exempts a man from responsibility for crime.

Chief Justice Shaw of Massachusetts, one of the ablest jurists this country ever produced, in an important and much-discussed case, stated the law, and it seems to me with great perspicuity and accuracy, in the following language: "The ordinary presumption is, that a person is of sound mind until the contrary appears: and in order to shield one from criminal responsibility, the presumption must be rebutted by proof of the contrary, satisfactory to the jury.

" In order to constitute a crime, a person must have intel
ligence and capacity enough to have a criminal intent and
purpose ; and if his reason and mental powers are either so
deficient that he has no will, no conscience or controlling men
tal powers, or if through the overwhelming violence of mental
disease his intellectual power is for the time obliterated, he is
not a responsible agent, and is not punishable for criminal
acts.

"The difficulty lies between those extremes, in the cases of
partial insanity, where the mind may be clouded or weakened,
but not incapable of remembering, reasoning and judging, or
so prevented by insane delusion as to act under false impres
sions and inferences. In these cases the rule of law is this :
a man is not to be excused from responsibility, if he has capacity and reason sufficient to enable him to distinguish between right and wrong as to the particular act he is then
doing ; a knowledge and consciousness that the act he is do
ing is wrong and criminal, and will subject him to punishment.

"On the contrary, although he may be laboring under par
tial insanity, if he still understands the nature and character
of his act, and its consequences ; if he has a knowledge that it
is wrong and criminal, and a mental power sufficient to apply
that knowledge to his own act, and to know that if he does
the act he will do wrong and receive punishment, such partial
insanity is not sufficient to exempt him from responsibility for
criminal acts.   *   *   *

" Monomania may operate as an excuse for a criminal act
in one of two modes.   1.   Either the delusion is such that the
person under its influence has a real and firm belief in some
fact, not true in itself, but which if it were true would excuse
his act.   2.   Or this state of delusion indicates to an experienced person, that the mind is in a diseased state ; that the
known tendency of that diseased state of the mind is to break
out into sudden paroxysms of violence towards friend or foe
indiscriminately ; so that the act was the result of the disease

and not of a mind capable of choosing : in short, that it was
the result of uncontrollable impulse, and not the act of a person acted upon by motives, and governed by the will."
(*Com. v. Rogers.* 7 *Met.* 501.)

An eminent judge in New York, in the highest court of
that state, has likewise given a definition which seems to me
worth reading :

"The insanity must be such as to deprive the party
charged with crime, of the use of reason in regard to the
act done. He may be deranged on other subjects, but if capa
ble of distinguishing between right and wrong in the particu
lar act done by him, he is justly liable to be punished as a
criminal.

" Partial insanity is not necessarily an excuse for crime,
and can only be so where it deprives the party of his reason
in the act charged to be criminal." (*Freeman v. The People,*
4 *Den.* 29.)

And a judge of the highest court of Pennsylvania, has in a
very condensed way stated the point thus : "The true test in
all cases lies in the word *power.* Has the defendant in a
criminal case the power to distinguish right from wrong, and
the power to adhere to the right and avoid the wrong."
(*Com. v. Haskell,* 3 *Brews.* 401.)

Now if I were to read you the judgment of many other
courts of high authority on this subject, which might be ad
duced, I should probably add nothing to the presentation of
the rule of law, as given in these extracts. And you will de
duce from these, first, that the inquiry starts with the pre
sumption that every man is sane until the contrary is proved
And next, that where the insanity is so far partial and limited
as to fairly raise the question whether it ought to be a defence
against a prosecution for an otherwise criminal act, the test is :
did it extend far enough over the faculties of the mind to take
away from the man that sense or consciousness of right or
wrong which rational beings possess ? So that if he did know

when he was setting the torch to the building, or drawing the weapon against his brother's life, that he was setting the fire or that he was taking life, he thought he was doing right, and was incapable of perceiving that he was doing wrong.

As I said a little while ago, even this exemption has grown up in the common law, as the whole knowledge, learning and treatment of insanity have grown up, within a comparatively recent period. In 1812, as you will doubtless remember, the Prime Minister of England, Mr. Spencer Percival, was shot dead in the lobby of the House of Commons, as he was going in to attend a session of Parliament, by a man named Belling ham. Of course the act produced a profound sensation, and Bellingham was not only hanged but dissected, within eight days after the murder. Justice or injustice, whichever it was, had in his case a speedy course. Now that man was unques tionably insane. It is conceded now, it was measurably con ceded then, that he was insane to the extent that would at the present day have acquitted him. He was under the delu sion that the British government owed him a very large sum of money. All his efforts to get attention to his claim were disregarded. He got into the state of mind that it seemed to him that murder was his legal redress. He could not sue the government of Great Britain. He thought the way to get justice was to kill the Prime Minister, and then in the inquiry that would naturally follow, it would come out that he was in the right—that this great claim was justly due him, and that he could get no attention to it in any other way. It was, in his delusion, the legal way to get justice. He was going to plead the claim in offset to the murder. Yet as great a law yer as Sir Samuel Romilly, one of the most philosophical of English jurists, said in connection with that case, at the time of it : "No person can have heard what the conduct and demeanor of this man have been since he committed the crime, or can have read his defence, without being satisfied that he is mad. But it is a species of madness which probably for the security of mankind ought not to exempt a man from being answerable for his actions." And Lord Eldon, then at the head of the judicial department of the British government, assumed that statement to be, as it probably was at that time, the law of Great Britain; and that in order to exempt a man from criminal responsibility for his acts, he must be such a total and complete maniac, as to have no knowledge or consciousness at all of what he was doing. You will see how the law has progressed towards the side of humanity and mercy. You see the difference between the law as stated by Sir Samuel Romilly, and the law as stated by Chief Justice Shaw. But when you look over the field of judicial proceedings on this subject since those dates, and perceive how terribly the modern and humane rule has been abused and misapplied; what a shelter it has proved for assassins; how many innocent lives it has cost to save the guilty lives of the murderers; you will see, also, that much is to be said after all in favor of the idea that prevailed at the beginning of the present century. It is by no means a question that has but one side; and only that the weight of that humanity and mercy, that temper the law more and more as civilization goes on, is cast into the scale, the strength of the argument might be on the other side. Leaving the assassin himself out of the question, and looking only as Romilly did, to the interests of society, it might not be difficult to reach the conclusion, that when a man is sane enough to set deliberately about the consummation of an assassination, it is better that he should pass into another world, where he will do less harm, and experience greater charity.

The question then is, in all cases of insanity, does the delusion which always accompanies it, and which indeed constitutes insanity, extend far enough to involve the whole operation of the mind? If not, does it extend far enough to destroy the consciousness of right and wrong, or the power to discriminate between them, in the particular transaction in question. And you will perceive that one of the learned judges

from whom I have read, lays stress upon the consideration,
whether or not an existing delusion connects itself with the
act. A man may be somewhat deranged on certain topics:
he may have certain ideas that are delusions, and that cannot be
accounted for except on the ground of mental disease, al
though upon other topics he is rational. He goes and kills a
person for his money, under circumstances totally disconnected
with the subject of his delusion. Now that man is partially
insane, no doubt. Shall he be acquitted? Very plainly not. If
his delusion is a monomania, or if it is a partial insanity only,
it must connect itself with the transaction, whatever it is, that
is in question, far enough to disable or destroy the conscious
ness of right and wrong, and the power of resistance in that
particular case.

I have thus tried to place before you the true rule, the
clear, simple, safe, salutary, intelligible rule of the law: the
rule that ought to prevail, and, whether it ought or not, does
prevail in courts of justice, when justice is done. I shall call
your attention hereafter to what may be called the sham in-
sanities, that have produced the scandalous results I have
referred to. The real insanity, which is my subject to day,
the insanity that does exempt and ought to exempt from crim
inal responsibility and to which the aid of every man, physician
or layman, should be cheerfully extended when it is necessary,
is that insanity which takes away the moral sense and conscious
ness which the Almighty has given us to keep us out of crime,
as long as we have possession of our faculties, and retain the
capacity to know that the thing is wrong, and that it has ulte-
rior consequences. And the last remark I have to make to day,
is that the defence of insanity, which is all that unfortunate
class has to rely upon, and constitutes their sole appeal to
the mercy and justice of their fellow beings when they have
committed some offence for which they are not really respon
sible, is brought into ridicule and contempt, and very largely
destroyed, by those who may be said to steal the livery of

insanity to serve the devil in. Such men are not only robbing
public justice, they are robbing the really innocent. More
than one case has occurred, where men have been prosecuted
for offences for which by reason of insanity they should not
have been convicted. To their defence a jury have replied:
"We have heard enough of insanity; it comes up too often, it
acquits too many murderers; we do not believe in it." And if
there were no better reason to be given, why every man, and
above all every physician, should set his face against any and
every attempt to abuse that plea, it should be found in the
consideration due to those who may be entitled to rely upon
it, and who have no other resort.

LECTURE IV.

INSANITY.

(Continued.)

I continue to day, gentlemen, the subject commenced on Friday last, of insanity as constituting a defence in prosecution, for criminal offences. I had gone so far as to try to point out with such distinctness as I hope may enable you to comprehend and remember it, the legal definition of insanity. Whether or not it is a correct medical definition, it is the standard to which all evidence in courts must be addressed. And I endeavored to make it clear, that the test in any given case, on the question whether a man was so insane at the time he committed an offence that otherwise would be criminal in its character, as to be exempt from responsibility, was wheth er at that time he was capable of distinguishing the right from the wrong in respect to that particular transaction—to know that what he was doing was wrong, and would subject him to punishment. And I re-state the point in order to add what perhaps I did not bring out with sufficient clearness, a dis tinction that some writers dwell upon, but which upon reflection will be perceived to be a distinction without a difference, that a criminal act, as a homicide or an assault, may be committed un der such sudden and uncontrollable—physically uncontrollable —impulse, that there is no special consciousness on the subject at the time by the party, though generally he may be quite able to distinguish right from wrong. Insanity sometimes shows itself in those sudden paroxysms, that might cause a man to throw himself upon his friend without any motive,—without any reason.—simply because he stands in the way ; just as a simi lar uncontrollable impulse might cause one who had no desire to commit suicide, to throw himself out of a window, or into a body of water. But you will see, that is after all, stating the same thing in other words. The test is the consciousness of right and wrong *at the time* of the act, and in respect to the act ; and although the man may be in such a condition that ordinarily he perfectly comprehends the character and conse quences of it, still he may be attacked with such a paroxysm, that he will commit the offence without at the time being con scious of either, acted upon, not by a mental motive, but by an irresistible physical impulse. It is probable that this form of insanity is very rare ; it is altogether too rare to be likely to occur for the first time on the occasion of committing the par ticular crime. Still it is a possible form, and it is a form that, as you may remember, Chief Justice Shaw referred to, in the opinion I read from.

Now, I want to call your attention to the different forms of spurious insanity that are brought forward in courts of law as an excuse for crime ; generally, though not always, the crime of murder : the forms of what may be called the insanity of the assassin, invented for the purposes of his defence. If you give attention to cases of that sort, you will find that they gener ally resolve themselves into two classes. There are two theo ries of what may be called spurious insanity. One is what is termed "partial moral insanity," affecting the conduct of the criminal not merely in respect to the particular act with which he is charged, but with respect to other acts of the same character. It is not claimed that he was insane only when he committed that particular murder or that particular larceny. The theory, is that he was afflicted with such moral perversion, propensity or proclivity, that he was uncontrolla-

bly impelled toward the commission of that offence, not in that
instance merely, but habitually. The other theory, which I
believe belongs exclusively to the crime of murder, and, sin
gularly enough, manifests itself in no other way, is what is
called "emotional insanity," a sudden insanity that attacks a
man and induces him to commit a particular offence, lasts
just long enough for him to commit it, and is caused by the in
tense desire or strong motive he has to do it. I have a few
words to say in respect to both of those classes of pretended
insanity, and I think you will perceive upon very little reflec
tion, that neither of them can survive a clear statement of the
theory upon which it rests; and that they are just as much
opposed to common sense, and common justice, and medical
truth, as I shall try to show you they are to the true law of the
land. One might well be surprised that any time should be
taken in refuting what in the abstract seems so little to need
refutation, if these theories had not been set up often enough,
and sometimes with sufficient success, to become a reproach to
public justice, and a danger to human life. Elaborate treatises
claiming the weight of authority, respectable, at least, in the
source from which they come, have been put forth in behalf of
them, not as being the law of the land, but as being what
ought to be the law of the land : and claiming, therefore, that
the law should be strained and twisted as far as possible,
so as to make it in its application to actual cases, what it is
claimed it ought to be.

The theory upon which the defence of this modern notion
of moral insanity proceeds, is that it is not a perversion of the
intellect, of the mental faculties, the perceptions, the reason
ing powers, or the memory. Its friends concede that the
subject may have as clear an intellectual or mental perception
of right or wrong in respect to the offence and its legal conse
quences, and moral consequences, as any one else of his grade ;
that he may be able to understand, and even discuss, the ques
tion fairly. But he is affected from birth with such a deficiency

of moral power, that when the time comes for the application
of the idea of right or wrong to the case, he is unable to resist
doing what he knows to be wrong, and to be punishable. A
man steals a watch. His defence is : "I am insane ; I can not
help stealing ; when I see property before me that is desirable
I can not resist the propensity to take it. In proof of that, I
can show you that this is not my first offence ; I have stolen
many times before, so that you see I intended no particular
injustice or wrong to the owner of this property ; I treat him
as I do everybody else, when I have the chance ; I am entitled
to be acquitted, and, of course, when I go out I shall con
tinue my career—a legally licensed thief, not amenable to the
law."

The great mass of mankind in civilized and enlightened
communities, whatever vices and faults they may be guilty of,
are not criminals : they do no commit the class of offences
known to the law as crime. Those who commit crimes are
the exception to the general rule. Why do not people gener
ally commit these offences ? For two reasons : in the first
place, their conscience, their sense of abstract right and wrong,
and duty, and their feeling of the degradation of crime are such,
that right minded men would be kept from it if they could be
positively assured that no consequences would follow, and that
they never would be detected ; and in the next place, a man of
sound judgment, and who can discriminate between what is
good policy and what is bad, knows that crime would be the
most foolish and dangerous thing he could engage in, even if
he had no moral scruples about it. Both conscience and
judgment are therefore a restraint, in the ordinary man,
against the commission of crime. No man ever deliberately
committed a crime unless the motive to do it was strong
enough to surmount both these forces ; till the anxiety for the
money, or to be revenged for an injury, or to re-
move somebody who stood in his way, became too strong
for his conscience, and too strong for his sound judgment.

Then, it may be safely enough said, that no man ever committed a deliberate crime, unless he had to a certain extent a diseased moral sense, or a will not strong enough to resist temptation to do what he knew to be both wrong and unwise. Men of sound, well-balanced, healthy minds do not commit crime. If they were the only persons amenable to justice and responsibility for crime, then, the criminal courts might be shut up. It is plain, therefore, that when a man comes before you whose body is well enough, and whose mind is well enough, but who seeks immunity on the score of diseased moral propensity to commit any kind of offence, he is simply only multiplying in his own case by repeated instances, what must be equally true of any intelligent person who was ever drawn into the commission of deliberate crime.

The truth is, and I venture to submit this proposition to the criticism of my medical brethren, as well as to that of lawyers, insanity is not a psychological affection: it is a pathological one. It is disease, and cannot be separated from disease. I do not believe that there ever was an unsound mind in a perfectly sound body; where insanity exists, it is the result of disease or injury in some form or other. It is said that insanity may be brought on by mental trouble, solicitude, anxiety, excitement, great fright, etc. But how many other diseases are produced, especially in the case of a system prepared for their reception, in the same way? How many bodily ailments that you are called to treat, may be traced to the original cause of mental trouble and solicitude? That does not prove that insanity is the direct result of the phenomena of mental consciousness. It only shows that such cause may act upon the body till it produces a disease of the brain, and the disease then affects the mind. Where there is a disease of the brain it is ordinarily accompanied with physical symptoms that you can perceive, though, perhaps, not always. Often the brain, I doubt not, on dissection would exhibit the disease; sometimes, I presume, it might not. Still, it must exist

there. when insanity exists. But even were this not true, and
if insanity can exist in the mind, without bodily affection, it
could not exist in the moral character, while the intellect remains intact. I reject altogether, therefore, and believe that
your subsequent experience will lead you to agree with me, this
theory of moral insanity, as having no foundation in medical
science nor in moral science, and as being directly opposed to
the law of the land, under which alone society can be protected.
'And any theory to the contrary amounts to this: that the criminal may go at large and continue his offences, if he can only
show to the satisfaction of the jury, that his propensity to do
so is unusually strong.

I am quite aware, and this is the last observation I have
to make upon this branch of the subject. I am quite aware
that paupers and criminals beget paupers and criminals. I
know very well how much early education, association, example, training and care have to do in protecting men from
crime, or drawing them into it. I know that men may, so to
speak, be born to crime, nurtured in crime, and so brutalized
by crime as to have apparently no moral sense, no adequate
power of resistance to temptation, and no sufficient control
over their passions. Crime with these unfortunates becomes
habitual, and almost a second nature. The subject may well
engage the consideration and the efforts of the humanitarian,
the philanthropist, and the law-maker. I would go as far as
any one in efforts to let light into the dark places, and ventila-
tion into the dung-hills of society, and in sympathy for their
unhappy and unfortunate denizens.

That subject stands by itself. When we come to the
question of the administration of criminal justice, which deals
rather with the interests of society than with the criminal,
these palliating considerations cannot be entered upon. How
much the Almighty Beneficence may condone in the conduct
of the criminal, in view of his disadvantages, it is not for us to
say; nor even what allowance we might ourselves make if we

were sitting only in moral judgment upon him. Legal judg
ment is a different thing; and that must be brought to the arbi
trary, the relentless, but after all the salutary and clear standard
of the law, that distinguishes between the man who commits
crime with a criminal motive, knowing better than to do it, and
the poor victim of mania who is drawn into it under a delusion
that makes it seem to him to be right, or under an uncontrol
lable physical impulse that he cannot resist. And to argue
that a man whose mental powers are unimpaired, may still be
exempt from punishment for crime because he inherits a moral
proclivity to commit it, is to my mind as absurd as to claim
that a pauper must necessarily be maintained in idleness, be
cause he inherits an irresistible propensity to avoid labor, and
to be supported by the town.

Now a few words as to the other form of spurious insa
nity, which I hope may some time be driven out of courts of
justice, "sudden temporary emotional insanity," arising only
in cases of murder. A man could not steal a horse under the
influence of that species of insanity, and expect that his defence
would be received with much respect. It is only in cases of
murder that it is available. The theory of "emotional insanity"
is precisely this : and when it is stated, very little can be add
ed by way of refutation ; it carries its own refutation with it :
that a man who never was insane in his life, and has no bodily
disease or mental perversion, may suddenly become insane for
the purpose of killing a particular personal enemy ; the cause
of his insanity is his intense desire and strong motive to kill
him ; the duration of it is just the time it takes to strike the
blow : its only manifestation is the murder ; it comes suddenly,
it goes as suddenly : it has no antecedent, it has no conse
quence, it has no accompaniment : it never returns. That is
emotional or paroxysmal insanity. A man becomes intensely
enraged against his neighbor. He has sustained, or believes
he has sustained a very great injury from him. He is anxious
to kill him. He goes about it with coolness and deliberation·

and does kill him. And the theory is, that having made all his preparations and sought out his victim, just before he struck the fatal blow he became insane for the first time in his life, and the moment after it was done he returned to permanent sanity.

In the miracles of the New Testament, relied upon to show the supernatural and divine power of their Author, we find some precedents of that sort, where the sick were enabled suddenly to rise up and walk, where the devil of insanity departed from a man suddenly, and as suddenly invaded some other body. Those are miracles, and when their truth is established, they are accepted as proof of miraculous power. Disease does not invade the human frame in that way, and it does not leave it in that way. You are not able to say to your patients, "rise up and walk," but only "rise up in due time, after taking pro per means." Nobody believes in this form of insanity in the abstract. It is not even believed in the concrete, when it is applied to the particular case. The physicians who permit themselves to say what little they can say with truth in favor of it, and the very jurymen who adopt it, do not believe it. They accept it as an excuse for justifying what the law does not justify. It has been very commonly applied to cases of seduction, where husbands or brothers go deliberately and coolly, seek out the offender, and kill him. The law does not justify such redress, and when the homicide is prosecuted, he must bring forward some other defence than the mere provocation, however great. Perhaps the case is one that evokes personal sympathy. Then makes its appearance this theory of "emotional insanity," that never occurs unless wanted for that purpose. Now, if it is desired to make it the law of the land that such offences shall be redressed by homicide, let it be made so by statute. That is not the question with which we are at present concerned. But the result never should be reached, by means that cast reproach and disgrace upon the public law of the land, as well as upon medical science.

This form of insanity was first invented in the celebrated
Sickles case, tried in Washington, many years since,—one
of the most cold blooded of assassinations, and as utterly desti
tute even of those circumstances that sometimes palliate homi
cide, as any murder that ever occurred. The assassin was ac
quitted on the score of insanity; an insanity of momentary
duration. There was a case in Kentucky, a little while ago, in
which a man dissatisfied with the decision that the Supreme
Court of that State had rendered in a case in which he was
interested, took his gun and shot the judge as he came off the
bench; and he has been acquitted on the score of "emotional
temporary insanity." There have been a number of cases of
that kind: and I challenge the production of one, in which
the defence has not been subsequently seen and conceded by
all men, to have been a pretence and a lie.

The duty of the medical profession in respect to cases of
that sort, to discriminate properly, and to stand by their dis
crimination, seems to me to be plain and to be important. You
may talk about mental trouble inducing insanity by acting upon
the brain until it produces disease. That is a tenable ground.
Domestic troubles may as well be the origin of such disease,
as any other mental troubles. But the distinction still remains
plain and clear between the man who commits a murder from
the intensity of the motive, and the man who commits it because
he is past the influence of a rational motive, or is incapable of
having any motive at all. In these cases the criminal not only
has a motive, a deliberate one, a rational one, but acts under
the influence of it, and that motive is all there is of his insanity.

You may probably be called upon when such emergencies
occur, to back up to a greater or less extent this theory. If you
should ever be brought to that conclusion, and should state in
reply to the usual preliminary enquiry, that you obtained your
education at the University of Vermont, I beg you will do the
University the justice to add, that what you are about to state
is in direct opposition to what you were there taught.

Now a few words by way of recapitulation is all I have to add, to day. The whole legal doctrine of the subject may be stated to be this. Insanity is a defence against the charge of any crime. A man is presumed, when he commits a crime, to be sane, until the contrary is shown. If he never had any fac ulties, like the idiot or the imbecile, or if he has lost them, as in the case of dementia, or if he is the victim of general mania, or what may be called total insanity, or if he is the subject of acute mania which from physical causes renders his conduct for the time being physically uncontrollable, in those cases it is very plain that he is entitled to exemption from responsibiilty. No particular medical skill is required to deal with them. They are patent to the common observer. Then when partial imbecility, or partial insanity is set up, the test that you have to apply is exactly this, and it is so clear that the common mind can understand it as well as the judge on the bench. In the first place, was the act committed under the influence of an uncontrollable physical impulse ; not an uncontrollable motive, which is a very different thing : the uncontrollable impulse that throws a man upon his friend, or upon any other person, without volition. Or if not, and the act was the result of delib erate, preconcerted, perhaps ingenious plan, of which lunatics sometimes are quite capable, in which the mind of the man, such as it was, operated, and which he considered, planned, remem_ bered, and understood, then was his mind so diseased, was he in other words under such mental delusion, that he did not know when he committed the offence, that in doing so he was doing wrong, and was amenable to punishment. Or was he at the time under a state of honest though deluded belief that he was doing right, as men have been who have sacrificed their children, believing they had a command from the Almighty to do so. Had the man at the time and in reference to the act, the power of distinguishing between right and wrong ; that is the legal test. It is upon this point your attention is to be concentrated. What definition you choose to give to insanity

in the abstract, aside from its judicial aspect, may be a totally
different matter. You may say that a man is insane when he
has a cold in his head, which to a certain extent benumbs his
faculties, if you think that is sound pathology, or correct
psychology. But the law has established a criterion for the
purposes of justice, that cannot be misunderstood, and ought
not to be disregarded.

LECTURE V.

INSANITY.

(Continued.)

Continuing, gentlemen, the subject of insanity, I have one further observation to add to what I said yesterday, in respect to criminal cases. Physicians are called upon to examine persons charged with crime, not only for the purpose of determining, or affording evidence by which the proper tribunal can determine, whether such person was insane at the time the offence was committed, but also sometimes, in order to ascertain whether he is sufficiently sane to be put upon his trial, which may be a very different question. In such cases experts are usually appointed by the court, and upon their report the question is decided by the court. In other cases, as I have said to you, they are selected and brought forward by the party who desires to use them. When a person is about to be put on trial, whether it is claimed that he was insane when the offence was committed or not, if it is claimed that he is then insane, the court directs an inquiry upon the subject, usually by the aid of medical experts, to settle that question preliminary to the trial : and the test to apply on such inquiry, is whether at that time, however he may have been before, which is of no consequence, except so far as it throws light upon his then condition, whether he is at that time mentally capable of comprehending the proceedings, and taking that in

7

telligent part in them, which is necessary to his defence; and
as you will see, the inquiry is a good deal easier and simpler
than when it is applied to a transaction that has passed by,
perhaps for a good while, and has been the subject of much
subsequent dispute.

Coming now to the second branch which I mentioned, of the
judicial aspect of insanity, I ask your attention for a few mo
ments to the effect of insanity upon civil contracts, or private
contracts between individuals. Although of less frequency of oc
currence, it is a very important topic, and sometimes attended
with considerable difficulty.

A person of unsound mind, within the definition I shall try
to give you, a person whom the law recognizes as being of un
sound mind, will generally be discharged by the courts, and
relieved from a certain class of contracts, called by lawyers exe
cutory contracts, that is, contracts to be performed in the
future, and that have not been consummated. While I do not
go into nice distinctions that would not be useful to you, the
general rule is, that the court will relieve the person of unsound
mind, from the consequences of such executory contracts. Then
as to contracts that have been performed, as a sale, for instance,
where the property has been delivered, the law will relieve
against such a contract under certain circumstances: where the
person is found to have been of unsound mind at the time of
the contract, and where the party with whom he dealt, either
knew, or in the exercise of reasonable attention and discretion
ought to have known, that the man was not in a mental condi
tion that rendered him capable of contracting. It has been
generally said that contracts of a simple and ordinary character
for necessaries, such as would be sustained against a minor, and
where it is obvious that no advantage has been taken of the
party, will be supported. Of course, this enquiry much depends
upon the nature and character of the contract itself, because
notice to the other side of the unsound condition of the mind
may be derived from the character of the contract. If it is

extravagant, unreasonable, unusual, or very unfair, that alone should put a man of ordinary sagacity upon inquiry, whether there is not something wrong in the mental condition of a man who proposes such a contract.

Now, the rule which courts apply in respect to the capacity to contract, and which in examinations for that purpose you should understand, is this: the unsoundness of mind, in order to affect a contract that is otherwise right, must be such as to deprive the party of the power of exercising ordinary and rational judgment in the transaction: either in comprehending the contract in its bearings, its consequences, or its relations, or in exercising in regard to those consequences and relations, the ordinary judgment of mankind. When that is found to exist, then arises, in the case of executed contracts, the further question, on which the medical expert may often be able to throw light, whether the other party knew or had good reason to know of this mental defect; and while, as I have said, it may be inferred in whole or in part from the character of the contract itself, if it was an unreasonable one, it may also be impor tant to know whether the party making the contract afforded that external evidence in his own person, in his manner, speech or deportment, that ought to have indicated to a person of ordi nary understanding, that there was unsoundness of mind. So both these questions may be presented to you: In the first place, was the person of sound mind within the legal defini tion; and if he was, did that insanity or imbecility manifest it-self in such a manner, that it should have put the opposite party on his guard.

Of course those who have much to do with the insane, learn that while sometimes the manifestations of insanity are very obvious, and cannot be overlooked, on the other hand they are sometimes extremely subtle, so that a long, patient and skilful examination may be necessary to detect them. There is a story told of a lunatic who was examined in an English court, in an action where the lunatic was exceedingly

anxious, and very cunning in his anxiety, to avoid being
found insane. It was a trial of intellect and of wits between
him and the eminent counsel who examined him over a period
of a day or two, upon all conceivable subjects, and the
counsel was about giving it up in despair, unable to bring out
a single trace of mental weakness. The lunatic was a man of
education and ability, and on all subjects the counsel had start
ed, he had elicited not only rational but often most interesting
replies. After a while a person in the audience passed to the
counsel a slip of paper on which was written "Try him on Eze
kiel." The counsel proceeded to introduce the subject of the
writings of the prophet Ezekiel, and to express his own opinion
in regard to them. "Why," said the man, "I am very glad to
hear you say that. *I am Ezekiel!*" That was his delusion :
a delusion pervading the whole constitution of his mind : a
monomania, that might as well have been a total mania, for all
practical purposes, and yet during several days he had eluded
all effort of a skilful examination, to induce him to say a word
that would raise the suspicion of insanity.

One other remark on the subject of contracts, as affected
by mental condition ; where a person is not of unsound mind
according to the criterion I have stated, and is quite capable of
doing ordinary business, but still is mentally impaired or
weakened, so as not to stand on a par with men of ordinary
judgment, and not to be a match for a sharp or unscrupulous
man in making a bargain, the contract of such a person will
often be set aside by a court of equity, when it appears that it
was an unfair and plainly unrighteous contract, and that an
unjust advantage had been taken of the mental condition of
the person entering into it. Here, then, another inquiry
arises : not whether a person is of unsound mind, or incapable
of doing business, but whether his mind was so far enfeebled
or affected, as to place him on a disparity with the man who
dealt with him in an important matter, and who took advantage
of this disparity. That, as you see, raises a much easier question,

because it is altogether easier to determine whether the mind is somewhat impaired, than it is to determine whether the degree of that affection comes up to the standard which the rule of law requires.

The third topic in this connection, is the effect of insanity upon guardianship proceedings : the duty of the judicial authority, at the instance of a party in interest, of placing a person under guardianship, because he is insane. And that, as you will see, involves two very important rights. One is the taking from him the custody and control of his own property, and the other is investing the guardian, as the law does in such cases, with the power of confining in an asylum the person who is adjudged insane. It involves, therefore, both property and liberty ; and there is no subject which gives rise to more bitter controversies in courts of law than this. When the insane person has recovered, or has partially recovered, he may apply to discharge the guardianship proceedings, and to exempt himself from further restraint. And not infrequently, actions for damages are brought by such a person, against those who have been concerned in confining him in an asylum.

Let me advise you, in the first place, in the course of your medical experience, never to have anything to do in a profes. sional capacity, or in any other capacity for that matter, with depriving a man of his liberty on the ground of insanity, if he is of full age, without the safeguard of proper legal proceed ings, and the appointment of a guardian over him. That proceeding, if it is sustained by the court, and a guardian appointed, protects those who act under it. You are protected in advising that a man should be sent to an asylum, or that he should be kept there and not discharged, and that the con trol of his property should be taken away from him, when the proper court of the country has appointed a guardian, and proceedings are taken by the guardian under his official responsibility ; assuming, of course, always, that such proceed-ings are in good faith.

When the question is presented to a medical witness as to the propriety of a guardianship, a different criterion of insanity from those that I have tried to point out as applicable to criminal cases and to contracts, arises : and that is, whether the man in general, not in respect to a particular contract or transaction, or a particular crime, but generally, is or is not capable of transacting ordinary business with ordinary judg ment : whether he had in the beginning faculties enough, and if he had, whether they have been so impaired by any in tervening cause, as to deprive him of that capacity. When this question arises as to particular contracts, the contract itself may be the guide. If it is a simple and easy one, it may not re quire much capacity. If it is difficult and important, with many bearings, a much higher standard is requisite. But in respect to guardianship proceedings, a broader and more general test must be applied, involving in its scope all the ordinary busi ness of life.

In respect to the propriety of advising confinement in an asylum, which is sometimes a difficult and delicate question, and ought always to be approached with caution, three consi derations are to be principally observed. *First*, the restraint of the patient, if his insanity renders him dangerous. Con finement in such a case is a necessity. *Second*, his cure, if he is not past cure, as recent cases, at least, rarely are. Whether this can be better accomplished in an asylum, may depend largely on the circumstances of the patient, and his means of commanding adequate private attendance at home. *Third*, the finding of a proper home for him, though incurable, and not dangerous, if, as in many cases, especially among the poorer classes, it can be obtained in no other proper way.

It is only upon one or more of these three grounds, that the confinement of the insane is morally justifiable, or ought ever to be resorted to. If but slightly insane, and not danger ous, even though incurable, or if entitled to homes where they can be safe, and have proper curative treatment and care,

they should no more be consigned to asylums to get rid of
them, than young children should be sent to the poor house or
the baby farm, to save the trouble or expense of their care.
Great and dangerous abuses have attended this subject, espe
cially in the detention of persons not insane, or who having
been insane, have recovered their reason. The responsibility
of advising in doubtful cases of that sort is grave, and may
not always be free from danger of liability.

I add nothing further on the subject of guardian
ship, except to say that in other cases, always in criminal
cases, often in cases of contract, the person supposed to be
insane, and standing upon the doubtful ground which leaves
room for discussion whether he is insane or not, is in favor of
establishing the insanity. If there is any pretence or simula
tion, it is in that direction. And on the other hand, when the
proposition is to deprive him of his property, or to shut him
up in an asylum, if he is not too insane to comprehend the
effect of the proceeding, he is on the other side. He is as anx
ious then to escape insanity, as in the other case to establish it.
You will thus encounter exactly opposite conditions in the two
cases.

Now, in regard to testing insanity, for all purposes for
which you may be called upon to test it, I may add some
suggestions that you may perhaps find useful. With the path
ology of the disease I have nothing to do. I cannot instruct
you in that. I have tried to point out the different criteria,
the tests and standards which the law applies. I do not think
it necessarily true, that physicians are the best judges, as they
certainly are not the sole judges, of the existence or degree of
insanity. I mean physicians who have not made that subject a
particular study, nor had in it a special experience. The physi
cian more than another is called on in such cases, for two rea
sons, perhaps three. In the first place, the visible physical
symptoms that almost always attend insanity, are of great im
portance in determining whether it exists ; and a physician, of

course, can discover and estimate those symptoms as no one
else can. Another reason is the power, or perhaps, rather the
habit than the power, of close, critical, personal observation,
which the physician cultivates and acquires, as few other men
do. The third is, that the physician may often have been the
family or attending physician of the subject, able to compare
him with himself, and to contrast his present physical and
mental condition with his former condition ; and familiar with
the history of his health, and with those predisposing causes
which may bear upon the inquiry. But after all, these are
only helps. You have to come down at last to dealing with
the mental phenomena, because those are what the question
finally turns on, in doubtful cases. What is the condition of
the mind? That can only be ascertained successfully, in diffi
cult and subtle cases, by very careful and repeated and saga
cious examination, by one taught to watch and weigh the
operations of the faculties of the mind. He has to contend in
some cases with the effort to seem to be insane, in another
class of cases with the effort to seem not to be insane, and in
a third class with a subject from whom little can be extracted,
who cares not whether he is pronounced insane or not, and is a
mere passive subject in the examiner's hands. Delusion, of
course, is sought for. What kind of delusion do you find?
On what subject? How far does it go? Is it important?
Does it invade the structure of the mind, or is it a mere sur
face eccentricity?

Men have often, marked peculiarities of disposition, and
strange idiosyncracies of character. They are habitually
moody, ill-tempered, morose, flighty, quick tempered, suspici
ous, secretive, very talkative, very reticent, disagreeable in vari
ous ways. They are what common people call "queer speci
mens," "crooked sticks," or, "a little cracked." These peculiarities
are easily magnified by interested or eager witnesses, and are
made to appear of more consequence in the telling than in
the observing. But this is not insanity in any legal sense of

the term. though sometimes indicating a tendency toward insanity, hereditary or otherwise. But whether you think proper to term it a mild or slight species of insanity or not, does not change its legal effect.

I may venture to say, that in the estimate and criticism of the purely mental phenomena of insanity, aside from its physical symptoms. the experienced lawyer is likely to aid you as much in determining that question, as you from your stand point. can aid him.

There are certain tests of insanity that are worth consideration in doubtful cases, and especially in cases where you have reason to suspect that it is simulated. You are called to a man who may or may not be insane. The first thing to attend to, is whether he has an interest to be insane, or not to be. Which side of the case is he on, if on either? Does he want to be insane. or does he insist that he is not insane? Then ascertain, if possible, what his hereditary tendencies are in that way. There is probably no affection or disease more likely to be hereditary, than insanity. I do not say certainly hereditary. but likely to be. It does not prove that a man is insane because his ancestors are. Often he may never be insane; and he may be insane in a very different way, or in a very different degree. But this is a very important step in the inquiry, when it can be settled one way or the other. Generally it requires an immediate disposing cause to bring it out. Sometimes, however, an hereditary insanity will manifest itself, where there is no direct apparent cause. or none that can be seen or learned. But a much slighter cause will develop hereditary insanity. than is necessary to produce it originally. The rule is the same that applies to many other diseases. which will attack certain constitutions and temperaments much more readily and easily. and upon much slighter cause, than others.

When it is ascertained whether there is or is not the hereditary tendency. then you should address yourself to the physical symptoms. And the cases of insanity are exceedingly rare, in

8

which a physician will not find the disease accompanied by perceptible bodily symptoms, that are not otherwise easy to account for. Those cannot be easily simulated, and therefore they are the more important. It belongs to another branch of your medical education to teach you to trace them, and follow them out.

Another preliminary inqury: has there been any imme diate or disposing cause that is adequate to produce the effect? Especially if no hereditary tendency exists : if it has appeared in the patient in the first instance, it must be the result of some adequate case. Has he been hurt? Has he had a sickness that might affect his brain? Has he been intemperate, or under such mental anxiety, solicitude, agitation, or excitement, as might account for the appearance of insanity? It is obvious that where you find a man with no hereditary tendency towards insanity, and no known immediate cause for it, and none of the physical symptoms that usually attend cases of insanity. you narrow the inquiry down to a very suspicious limit, and especially if it is a case where it is an object for the man to be thought insane. A strong circumstantial case is made out against the existence of the disease to start with, and yet one that is by no means necessarily conclusive. Insanity, though improbable, may still exist. The mental manifestations are then to be considered, which after all must be the ultimate test of a diseased mind.

Simulated mania almost always over-acts. Ignorant people who set out to appear insane, usually begin to be vio lent, and turbulent, and noisy: they shout, sing, jump, and con duct themselves in an extravagant manner. General mania often does exhibit itself in such uncontrollable, unaccountable, spasmodic violent conduct. The question then is, whether this is real mania? Whether the noise and disturbance is made in good faith, or whether it is manufactured for the occasion. Now there are two tests that in that class of mania very rarely fail. One is, that however it may be in the milder and partial

forms of insanity, it is always the case in these instances of
general mania, that the various physical symptoms are pro
nounced and unmistakable. When a man is a maniac, a
lunatic, in the common acceptation of the term, it is obvious in
his person, his pulse, his temperature, his eye, his skin, his
sleeplessness, his unnatural appetite, his want of appetite. All
of the physical functions will be more or less deranged, and
abnormal.

The other test is found in watching the patient when he
is not aware that he is seen. The acting he has been carrying
on, is then suspended, the violence subsides. Indeed it could
not be long kept up without some interval of rest. By these
means simulated general mania is usually easily detected.

The more troublesome cases arise, when the subject is
cunning enough to set up a partial mania, or, on the other hand,
where he has a partial mania, and is cunning enough to try to
conceal it. Where a partial mania is pretended, and the man
goes to work to manufacture it, it is almost always over-done,
unless he is very skilful on the subject of insanity. It is al
most always over-acted. He is too anxious to appear to be
insane. You see in the demeanor of the man, that he wants
you to perceive his delusion; he is not trying to conceal it, but
makes it as prominent as possible; he is inconsistent, and un
certain in his delusions, and does not stick to his text. In
ordinary cases of monomania, or partial mania, you will find the
patients are consistent and even logical in their delusions, and
the delusion is generally the same, at least for a consi
derable time, and excludes inconsistent delusions. You trace,
therefore, in simulated insanity, usually, the evidence of its
manufacture.

There is another indication, and I never saw a person
under the influence of partial mania, where it did not seem to
me I could detect it, and that is an indescribable look in the
eye, that conveys to you the idea, that the insane person, while
he adheres to his delusion, has still a lingering notion in his

mind that you do not believe it : a look, sometimes most pathetic and appealing, indicating a sort of undercurrent of thought unconsciously going on, as undercurrents sometimes go on in the human mind, that his delusion, so real to him, is not real to the spectator. This is something no one can simulate. The man who is anxious to make himself out insane, shows you the opposite. If he has any anxiety, it is an anxiety to see whether he has created an impression, whether he has made his point. The real lunatic only, seems to say mentally, in a sort of sad, mournful undertone, "Do you believe this? Do you see anything wrong in me? Do you think I am mistaken?" And I think one of the very best tests of insanity, is that look, which once seen by a thoughtful observer, will be remembered, and which can be a great deal better remembered than described.

No good, in my judgment, comes from theorizing on the legal or judicial aspect of insanity. Little benefit is derived either, from rehearsing the many cases, interesting, melancholy, or amusing, that the lunatic hospitals abound with, because every man's case has to be determined by itself. Physical symptoms, of course, as in other diseases, may be similar. Certain fixed principles, like that of the hereditary taint, can be recognized; but when you come to deal at last, with the pheno mena of the mind, it has pleased the Almighty to provide, that every man's mind shall have its own qualities and characteristics, as it has its own joys and sorrows : that it shall stand or fall in its own way, and be judged of here, as hereafter, on its own merits and its own consciousness.

LECTURE VI.

WILLS.

I shall ask your attention to day, gentlemen, to the sub
ject of the disposition of property by will, so far as physicians
may be expected to have anything to do with it ; and it is a
business with which physicians are likely to have a good deal
to do, in several ways. In the first place, when the question
arises as to the capacity of a person to make a will, who is
suffering with illness, enfeebled by old age, or, perhaps,
thought to be affected to some extent by insanity, the enquiry
is often addressed to a physician, and especially to an at
tending physician, who has been watching the case, whether
or not there is the mental capacity that justifies the attempt.
He is very likely, also, to be called on to be a witness to the
will. For some strange reason, the duty of making a will,
which ought always to be discharged in the vigor of life, is
very commonly postponed until the party is *in extremis.*
Men seem to think that making a will somehow accelerates
death, and is like ordering the coffin. Many wills are therefore executed from the sick and dying bed, and sometimes in
extreme old age. Of course the attending physician in such a
case, being on the spot, and being one of those with whom the
patient is familiar, and by whose presence he is not agitated,
and frequently being a friend of the family, is very naturally
called upon to act as a witness. And if the case is one where

although real capacity exists, any question could ever arise about
the validity of the instrument, it is extremely proper that the
attending physician, who, in addition to his general knowledge
of the subject, understands the patient's condition, should be
come one of the witnesses. Then, when the will has been
executed, and is challenged in a court of justice, and sought
to be broken, as the common phrase is, or set aside, on account
of the incapacity of the testator, the testimony of the physi
cian becomes very important, whether he is a subscriber to
the will or not ; especially important if he is a subscriber ;
and still more, perhaps, if he has been, also, the attending
physician. You will see, then, that this topic is one you will
be likely to encounter in your professional life, in more ways
than one. It is, therefore, necessary, or at least desirable, that
physicians should approach the subject with some general
knowledge of what the law requires, to enable a person
to make a valid will, and how it is to be executed. And I may
digress here far enough to say, that if some elementary in
struction on those general subjects of the common law, that are
involved all the time in the ordinary business of life, was more
common to all classes of students, they would find it extremely useful. It is like hygiene in the science of medicine,
not at all the exclusive property of the professional man.

Every person who has arrived at years of discretion, is
entitled by the law of our country to make a will, disposing of
his property ; and in making it, he can dispose of any and all
property he has, and he may dispose of it just as he pleases,
without regard to the claims of family, affection or propriety.
The subject is altogether in his own hands, as to any property
that will be left after •the payment of his just debts, with the
single exception of the claims of his wife, if he has one. Her
legal share, given her by the law, in the deceased husband's
property, cannot be taken away by him. And, therefore, if he
makes a will, and either does not provide for her, or makes a
provision that she is dissatisfied with, she has a right to have

her share taken out of the estate, before the will takes effect; to that extent, and to that extent, only, the law imposes a res triction upon the absolute power of every person owning pro perty, to dispose of it by will. In the state of Louisiana alone, in this country, so far as I know, as in the countries of Europe, where the civil law prevails, it is otherwise. There, children have certain rights in property by descent, which cannot be taken away by will.

Now to the validity of a will, there are four requisites. In the first place, the person that makes it, called the testator, or testatrix, must be of sound disposing mind and memory. That is the language in which the law conveys the idea of a sufficient mental capacity for this purpose. Secondly, the will must be written; and expressed with such clearness, that the court can find out from it what disposition of the property is really intended. They will go as far as possible in the con struction of a will, to carry out the intention of a testator, and no particular form of words is usually necessary; if with reasonable certainty they can ascertain from its language what the testator meant, they will carry the will into effect. The third requisite is, that the will must be signed by the testator or testatrix, and signed with the knowledge and intention that it is to operate as a will. That is to say, not under any mis take or imposition, but with full knowledge and assent, that the document is, and is to be, the will. And of course that implies, also, that it must be freely signed, in the exercise of the personal volition of the testator, and not under fear, com pulsion, or coercion: he must neither be cheated nor forced into signing it.

And the last requisite is, the requirement of the statute in this state, which is substantially the same in most of the states, although on this point the particular rules in different states vary somewhat—that the will must be at tested by the signature of three witnesses, who sign it in the presence of the testator and of each other, and who have seen the testator sign : so that the four parties to the will, the maker and the three witnesses, shall all see each other sign, the whole business being done on one occasion, when all are present. And all must understand that the object of attesting the document is to establish it as a will. I do not use the word "see" in its literal sense, because a blind person can make a will. It is only necessary that the testator who is blind shall be made aware that his signature, or whatever passes for it, is taking place in the presence of the witnesses, and that their signatures are being appended in his presence as an at testation of his will. And by signature, I mean such a signa ture as the party is able to make : a person who cannot write, may make his mark between the words of his name written by some other person : and so a person in extreme debility from illness or old age, may have his hand guided by some other person, and make such signature as he can in that way, if it is only understood and intended by him that it is the signature he would make by his own act, if he only had the physical ca pacity.

Nothing is more commonly misunderstood, and some times even in the legal profession, than the duty of the witness to a will. He is very generally regarded as being a mere witness to the signature, who, having seen the party sign, or having heard him say he has signed, adds his own name, because the law requires a witness, as a matter of form. This is a grave mistake. When the witnesses put their sig natures to the will, the law which has placed them there, re quires them to discharge a double and most important duty. First, to see that the signature of the testator is his genuine signature, and that he signs understanding the document to be a will, and not under any imposition, mistake, coercion or fear : and next, to satisfy themselves, as far as they reason ably can with the means and the opportunity they have, that the testator is at the time, of sufficient mental capacity. Until the witness is satisfied of that fact, he should not append his name ; because in legal effect, although it is not written out (probably it would be better if it were), he is certifying, not only that the signature of the testator is free, voluntary and intelligent, but, also, that when he made it he was of sufficient mental capacity. I have seen physicians in some instances, by not understanding the effect of their attestation, placed in a very unfavorable position, and a very disagreeable one.

٭. A physician was once called into court as a witness on the contest of a will, where the question was, whether the testator had capacity enough to make it, understandingly. The physician was one of the subscribing witnesses to the will, and testified that in his opinion the testator had not sufficient capacity. He was at once confronted with the inquiry, " Why then did you attest it ? Why did you sign a will and help to make it, if you were then to come here and testify that the maker had not proper capacity?" The truth was, the witness had never thought of that ; he put his name to the will because he was asked to ; he had his own opinion all the time as to the capacity of the testator ; and when he was asked to state his opinion in court, he did so. But his testimony provoked such criticism that it actually turned the case the other way : the jury deriving the idea, that his original opinion must have been such as to warrant him in the signing of the will, and that by some reason or other, he had been induced to alter it. And that is not the only instance I have seen of a subscribing witness ·placed in the same dilemma. In these cases the physicians were upright in intention, and intelligent in judgment, but were drawn into a false position, by not understanding in the outset, that when they put their names to the will, they were certifying, so far as they had the means of knowing, to the mental capacity of the testator.

When, therefore, you are called upon, as you will be, probably, many times, not only to determine the sometimes perplexing question of the capacity of a party to make a will, but to become a subscribing witness to it, bear in mind that

9

you are deciding not only an important inquiry, but one on which you may very likely be required to back up your opinion in a court of justice. So that if you have any serious doubt as to the capacity of the person to make the will, ex press that doubt frankly, and decline to put your name to the in strument. You may not be able, at the time, to institute such a thorough examination as would enable you to determine the question to your own satisfaction. But if there is any se rious doubt upon the subject, which you are not able to solve, or which there are not time and means of removing, it is better to keep out of the transaction, in view of its ultimate conse quences : because the law requires the subscribing witnesses always to be called, if living, when the will is offered for pro bate. If, notwithstanding your opinion, parties choose to go on and have the will made, it ceases to be any affair of yours. You are not the guardian of the testator, or required to see that a will is executed, or that it is not executed. You have nothing to do with it until you are invited to take part ; but if you are invited,—if your opinion is asked,—it should be so expressed, that if you are afterwards called to repeat it in a court of law, you will not be encountered by any incon sistency between what you say there, and what you have said before.

The rule of law in respect to the measure of mental capacity, in this as in the other cases to which I have had occasion to call your attention, establishes a clear and de finite criterion ; that is to say, just as clear and definite as a measure of the capacity of the human mind can be, when stated in words. And substantially it is this. The testator must have mind enough, perception, memory, reasoning power enough, to be able of himself, without any help, to call into his mind those who have natural claims upon him, and those who should be remembered and considered when he is making a will ; to call up also in his memory the property he has, what it is, where it is, and to determine by volition of his own, what he wishes to do with it. So that the disposition made, is the result of his own choice, rationally exercised, dealing with property and claimants, the knowledge of which is correctly recalled by his own memory. If he can do thus much, of himself, the instrument will stand, however failing or feeble the powers of mind or body may be. The standard, as you readily perceive, is not a high one. It re quires no very powerful exercise of the mental faculties. It does not even require so much vigor of intellect as would be necessary to the making of an ordinary contract, where an opposite contracting party has to be encountered.

It is not necessary that the disposition should be the wisest or the best. The question addressed to the triers, is not whether that is the will they would have made, if they had been in his situation, or would have advised him to make, if their opinion had been asked. If he had mind enough to make it of his own accord, his own volition, and his own adequate memory, the will is valid, and will be established.

Of course I do not mean to be understood that it makes no difference upon such an inquiry, what sort of will a man makes. That makes no difference after the instrument is once ascertained to be *his* will, rationally and voluntarily executed. The disposition of the property may be most objectionable, and unjust, and still be sustained, if legally made, in the ex ercise of such moderate capacity and volition as the law re quires. But very important and even decisive light is often thrown upon this question of capacity, by the character of the will itself. Is it reasonable? Is it probable? Is it consis tent with the affections, the wishes, the known previous intentions of the testator? Or is it, on the other hand, strange, inconsistent, unaccountable, as well as wrong? The answer to these inquiries may in itself sometimes turn the scale, and be sufficient to determine the question, whether or not the will was the result of mental capacity or incapacity, of sound ness or unsoundness of mind. But it is decisive only as far as it reaches and affects the cardinal point, the actual condition of the mind.

The law favors the disposition of property by will; it goes as far as it can in support of it, without crossing the confines that separate justice from injustice. The presumption is therefore in favor of capacity. When a will is presented, it is not necessary to prove that the maker was sane and competent; that is presumed until he is proved to have been incompetent. And a will legally executed, is valid until successfully impeached by proof.

Mental incapacity to make a will, may arise in three ways. First, from some of the forms of insanity; and you will remember that I forebore, in discussing the subject of insanity, generally, to speak of its effect upon the making of wills, because it may be considered with more propriety in this connection. It is a much easier task, usually, to determine doubtful questions of insanity as they affect the validity of wills, than in many other cases where they are involved, and especially where the physician has the opportunity to see the party at and before the time when the will is executed. The case is relieved in the first place, of all effort on the part of the testator to appear to be insane, or to appear not to be insane. He is usually acting calmly and thoughtfully, surrounded by his friends, doing what he has a right to do, and what no one has a right to prevent. Thus all theories of moral insanity, emotional insanity, and other spurious or imaginary forms of mental disease are out of the question, as these never attack a person who is engaged in a lawful act. Criminality, as we have before seen, is absolutely necessary to their existence. And finally, the judgment of the physician is formed at the time of the transaction in question, and not long afterwards, when it has perhaps become the subject of heated controversy, and wide diversity of statement as well as of opinion.

When a doubt arises as to the validity of a will, or the com
petency to make a will, on the ground of possible insanity, the
question is, first, does any delusion that is found to exist,
involve the whole structure and operation of the mind, so that
the man is really insane upon all subjects, and incapable of
natural mental action. Or if not, and there is found to be only
a delusion on one subject—a monomania—does that delusion or
mania in any way connect itself with the business of the dis
position of property, or with any of the individuals who ought
to be taken into consideration, or naturally would be taken
into consideration, in making it, such as wife or children. A
man may take up the delusion that his best friend is his worst
enemy : that this enemy is pursuing him by day and by night,
that he is seeking his life, that he is plotting against his hap
piness and his success in whatever he undertakes, and the
delusion may reach the degree of monomania, having no
foundation in fact, and no foundation in probability. While he
has no good reason to think so, yet he is tortured and tor
mented with the imaginary idea, that every where he encoun
ters the opposition of this enemy. So that he might even
meet that man under circumstances in which if he were to kill
him, he would be entitled to be acquitted on the ground of insanity. He would have done it in imaginary self-defence, in order
to protect himself against the fancied and imminent danger that
was menacing him. Such a person is of course insane—a mon
omaniac—and yet may perhaps be able to make a will that is
valid ; perhaps not. In his relations with his family, his wife,
his children, his connections, in the transaction of his ordi
nary pecuniary business, in knowing what his property is, what
becomes of it, and in having correct ideas as to what ought
to become of it, he may be sane and natural. So that the
will of that insane man—insane enough under a supposable
case to be acquitted in a court of justice if he committed a
homicide—might still be valid. But suppose, on the other
hand, that the person against whom this insane, morbid pre-

judice has arisen, were the wife, the son, the daughter of the
testator. When he makes a will his first and foremost idea is
naturally to exclude that wife or child from sharing in his
property—the child that has become his enemy, the wife who
is alienated from him. The delusion then touches the very
point in question, and that will cannot stand.

When the delusion is not so general as to involve the
whole mind, and to exclude the idea of natural mental action
on any subject, the question is, how far, if at all, does it reach
or attach to the matter of property, its situation, amount or
disposal, or the persons naturally or reasonably to be thought
of in making a will. And it is these cases of partial insanity or
monomania, sometimes very near the line, that give rise to the
most serious debate, and the greatest doubt, and that need to
be most intelligently considered.

Incapacity may also arise where there is no insanity, and
never has been, from the mere effects of acute disease. The
stupor of typhus, the delirium and excitement that attend
nervous diseases, and many other forms of illness, may place
the party where, for the time being, he is not capable of mak
ing a rational will of his own volition, although he has never
been afflicted with any mental disease. Those affections,
those sources of incapacity, are peculiarly and almost entirely
within the province of the physician. While the lawyer or the
intelligent layman may judge on the question of insanity
sometimes as well as the physician, or nearly so, if he has the
means of knowledge, when it comes to the distraction that
is born of immediate acute disease, the whole subject is'
within the domain of the physician.

Mental incapacity may arise also from old age ; because
the will is made too late : after nature has begun to shut up
the windows and the doors, and to put out the lights, in the
tenement which the soul is about to abandon. It may arise
from that cause alone ; where there is no particular illness, or
disease, and where there never has been anything like insani-

ty. So two or more of these causes may combine. A man may be insane in mind, and be also under the influence of acute disease; he may be of extremely advanced years, and likewise affected by illness; and he may possibly have all three of these disabilities at the same time, to a greater or less degree, and mental incapacity may come from a combination of them all.

Of course, as I had occasion to say in discussing the general subject of insanity, every case stands by itself. It must be judged by itself, and by its own peculiar manifestations. And the power of judging correctly must be acquired by experience and reflection. It will be best exercised always, when you can compare the man with himself; what he is, with what he has been.

There is another rule of law applicable to the disposition of property by will, that should be understood and borne in mind by those having to do with such transactions. Where a man is capable of making a will, according to the test that I have stated, where he comes up in capacity to the legal requisite that I have tried to explain, so that his will, if it was his own will, without any undue interference, would stand, that will may still fail. If he was so far impaired by disease, by old age, by any partial mental unsoundness; if his faculties are for any reason so far weakened that he is easily accessible to the improper influence of others, and cannot stand up in defence of his own wish and intentions as ordinary men do; then if what is known in the law as undue influence is brought to bear upon him, and a will is thus obtained that he would not have made if he were let alone, that will will be set aside. Not because he had not capacity to make any will, but because he had not capacity to do it when subjected to an improper, crowding and overpowering influence. I do not mean to say that no one has a right to interfere with the making of a will. A man has a legal right, whether delicate and judicious or not, to try to obtain by reasonable suggestions and persuasions, a will to be made in a particular way. He may ask a person who is about to make a will, to remember him, or to provide for another, and however indelicate it may be, there is nothing illegal about it. But when that pressure is carried beyond suggestions and fair request, to the degree which the law characterizes as undue influence ; when it becomes a pressure, a force sufficient with a weak man to over-balance what he would have done, or what he wanted to do ; where without strength to resist the importunity, he does what the by-stand er desires, and not what he desires himself, that disposition will be set aside.

You are called upon, let me suppose, to express an opin ion, or to participate as a witness in making the will of a man of whom you are satisfied, that if he was only let alone, he has capacity enough to make a will. He is weak, he is feeble, but he could make a will if let alone ; his mental powers come up to the legal standard, which, as you have seen, is not a high one. But he is surrounded by people who are capable of subjecting him to the sort of pressure that.I have described. How far they have done it, you do not know. It has not been done in your presence. It is just one of those cases, where assuming that the man has been fairly treated, the will would be well enough, but assuming that he has been pressed and crowded, it ought not to stand, and if that fact appears, it will not stand. Now it seems to me the duty of the medical man in such a case as that, to assent, if he pleases, to act as a wit ness to the will, protecting his assent, however, with a state- ment at the time of it, that he assumes the capacity to make the will because he assumes there has been no undue influence or interference. That leaves his position a consistent one, if he should be called afterwards as a witness to the will, and it should turn out that this sort of pressure had been going on to such an extent, as to operate upon the weak mind of the testator. By his signature attesting the will, he has asserted nothing more than his belief in the capacity of the maker of the will, under fair treatment. And it is not at all inconsistent with his afterwards expressing an opinion of what might be the result upon the testator, of undue and im proper interference.

I do not know that I can add anything further, usefully, upon this subject. You will see upon reflection how impor tant to yourselves as well as to others your connection with it may become, and how carefully it should be approached. Wills, as you know, give rise often to violent contests, to dis ruption of families, to bitter personal feelings, to great con trariety of opinion, and conflict of evidence. They may dispose of a great deal of property, in a very short time, by a very simple act: they may work great wrongs, they may work great good. And every witness, therefore, who is invited to partici pate in such a transaction, and above all the medical witness, and still more the medical witness who is attending the case, should bear these considerations in mind, and have a clear, distinct and definite idea of what he is about, and the right and the wrong of it, before any dispute arises, and before his opinion or motives can be laid open to criticism.

LECTURE VII.

FICTITIOUS INJURIES.

I have but little more than an apology for a lecture to offer you to-day, because I am compelled to treat the subject of it in a very imperfect manner. But what I have to say will at least have the merit that should belong to apologies, that of being brief. I wish to say something about what may be called fictitious injuries, and simulated, pretended diseases, claimed to have grown out of fictitious injuries. The difficulty of treating it from the legal stand-point is, that I can do little more than point out what you ought to learn, without doing much towards giving you the required instruction. I can but point the way. And I have been led by a sense of the deficient manner in which I am obliged to treat this and other subjects, strongly toward the conclusion, that lectures in this department ought to be, as I hope some day they will be, alternated between the lawyer and the physician, thus presenting both sides of a subject, which, as I pointed out to you before, has two distinct sides, the medical and the legal.

Probably the large majority of cases in which physicians are called in court to testify, are cases of personal injury, arising from some cause for which the law gives redress in the way of damages; from an assault, or from some one of an infinite variety of accidents, for which somebody is responsible, because somebody is to blame, actually or constructively.

Of course many of these cases, perhaps I should say most of them, are genuine claims—real injuries, and entitled to their suitable redress. That redress is altogether within the province of a jury. When a cause of action is once established in behalf of a person who has been injured, against another who is to blame for it, the amount that he shall recover is entirely in the hands of the jury. And this has become a very fruitful source, and I am sorry to say a rapidly increasing source, of fictitious claims, pretended or grossly exaggerated claims of injury, for the purpose of obtaining damages. And as insurance companies long ago found out that there is nothing so combustible as over-insurance, so lawyers have learned, that there is nothing so aggravating to personal injuries sustained by accident, or otherwise, as an existing claim for damages. It is astonishing how many cases of permanent injury arise, altogether and absolutely incurable, and it is astonishing how fast these cases recover their health, after they have first recovered adequate damages. The detection of this sort of claim has therefore become a very important duty, and it is of necessity wholly in the hands of physicians and surgeons. It may be called, perhaps, detective medicine, or the diagnosis of disease that does not exist; and as you see, nearly the whole business of such detection becomes the subject of medical and and not of legal science.

These claims have increased so much of late years, that they have begun to attract very great attention. Actions against towns, for injuries sustained by defects in the highways, which have always been given by our law hitherto, have recently been abolished in this state, and likewise in other states, on account of their abuse. Because the greatest good of the greatest number, which is the basis upon which laws are made, or ought to be, has come to require, that those entitled to compensation for such injuries should be deprived of it, rather than that the towns should be subjected to the exorbitant and outrageous claims that are so often made, and sometimes sustained. Railroad companies have also suffered very severely in cases of claims for injuries, that have been absolutely fictitious. Very large damages · have been recovered, too, in some cases against individuals, upon causes of action that have been equally unjust. The success of these speculations has brought reproach upon the courts, because so many cases of pretended permanent injuries get well when the suit is ended. And the ultimate result of the proceeding, presents the court in the aspect of a tribunal to execute injustice instead of justice.

Nothing has contributed so much to the advance of this system of deception, as one or two modern theories of injury, and of disease resulting from injury, that have found their way of late years into courts. The trouble with fictitious cases had formerly been, that there was nothing of the alleged injuries to be seen. When a man who pretended to be hurt went to his physician, there was no external indication of it, there was no fracture, no bruise, no deformity, no discolora tion, no swelling, nothing. Of course it is very difficult upon such a case as that, to predicate a serious or permanent injury, that ought to be redressed by large damages. I do not know which profession is entitled to the merit of the invention, but the idea was started not very many years ago, and within my own recollection, of putting these cases upon the ground of an injury to the spine, sufficient to produce a paralysis of the lower limbs, without any external appearance at all.

The theory of the injury, as it started out in the first place, was what they called a "partial concussion of the spinal mar row." A man meets with a small accident; nobody would suppose that he could be much hurt. Bye and bye, in the course of a few months, he begins to be paralyzed. It is a case of "partial concussion of the spinal marrow," devel oped long after the injury that caused it. I had the pleas ure, in a case tried in this city a number of years ago, of hear ing that theory so completely demolished by Dr. Darling,

your professor of anatomy, and one or two other eminent physicians, that it has not been heard of much, in this vicinity,
since. It was made to my unscientific comprehension very
plain, that if you knock a man down, he would be likely to fall
at once, and not come gradually to the ground about six
months afterwards. Still, I ought to say, that some respecta
ble medical authority was found in its favor. It did not
stand entirely without scientific support.

More recently that theory has taken another form : one
that is very ingenious and sometimes very successful. It
is that the injury claimed may have been sustained by the
nerves themselves, the vertebral nerves, which supply the
lower limbs, so that in course of time a paralysis takes place
of the leg, greater or less, in consequence of an injury that
cannot be seen at all. Now the advantage of this theory is,
that it may be true. That very thing may happen in a given
case. It was maintained by the best medical authorities, that
the other mode of injury could not happen in any such way
as was claimed. But there may be just such an injury as
the recent theory describes, and it may result in just such a
disease—a paralysis. This ground of action has had such
a run in England, that there has been a book written about
it by Dr. Erickson, who calls the disease "Railway Spine,"
because it so constantly attends railroad accidents, and is
so rarely seen disconnected with a suit for damages.
Dr. Erickson has shown by those statistics that are so
formidable when enough of them are brought together, that
while great numbers of passengers present at railway accidents, get the paralysis that comes from the injury to the
vertebral nerves, it almost never, perhaps never, attacks the
employees of railroads, the poor fellows who have no action
for damages, if they get hurt. The brakeman, the fireman,
the conductor, get hurt often enough, because they are very
much exposed. They never have that form of disease. But
you catch a passenger of the right sort, who is present at the

time of an accident, and you may reckon on paralysis, to a
dead certainty.

Now it is easy to see how physicians, and very respect
able physicians, are drawn into giving support to theories of
this kind, that in the abstract, and in the light of statistics,
certainly appear absurd. No physician is called upon by
a man who proposes that he should help commit a fraud.
The proposition would be an insult. The physician is sent
for to attend the case medically, and nothing is said about
damages. The patient is very much afflicted: he is in
pain; he is incapacitated: he wants help. It does not
occur to the doctor that the man is shutting himself up, and
paying surgeons' bills, for the sake of pretending to be hurt.
He believes the symptoms that are detailed to him by his
patient, and of course looks for the cause that has brought him
into this situation. So he traces back, and starts the best
theory he can to account for the existing result, that must
have had some cause. The patient conveniently develops
symptoms that he finds the doctor is looking for. The physician gets interested in the case. Bye and bye there is a
lawsuit. The physician's theory is attacked on the other side.
Other medical men are brought in, who examine the patient
from a different stand point, and with the suspicion that the
claim is a fraud. The doctor who attended the case, and who
started the theory, becomes naturally excited by the sugges
tion that he has been cheated, and some of his friends are
called in: they perceive the same symptoms that he did, hear
his statement, and naturally take his side: the other side is
reinforced by new physicians: the respective counsel get very
much in earnest: in short, it becomes "a very pretty quarrel as
it stands." And the jury, who know nothing at all about the
subject of such an injury—twelve honest men, selected because
they have no education that enables them to know anything
about it, have finally to decide the case the best way they can.
upon the conflicting medical evidence, and generally dispose

of it in favor of the most popular party, or the most ingenious or eloquent advocate.

Counsel are quite as liable to be deceived in such cases as physicians are. I remember being concerned in a cause where a woman who had met with an accident on the highway, and had been thrown out of a wagon, had a miscarriage immediately afterwards, and was reduced to the point of death. She recovered, and brought an action against the town, in which her husband joined. They were all strangers to me, the transaction having occurred in a distant county, but had the appearance of being respectable people, and I became much interested in her case. It seemed to me a very hard one, and especially as the town set up the defence that the claim was a deception and a fraud. She recovered a considerable judgment; and afterward it came out, as the fact was, that at the time of the accident she was driving home from an operation that had been performed upon her, for the purpose of producing an abortion. She met with this accident on the way home, by a defect of the road, but the subsequent miscarriage, which was the principal foundation for the claim for damages, was, of course, the consequence of the operation and not of the accident. The counsel were taken in, the phy'sicians were taken in, great injustice was done, and yet I do not know that either physicians or counsel on the side of the woman, could be blamed for the result.

The ingenuity and persistence with which deceptions of this sort are often maintained, is surprising. And very close and sometimes extended observation on the part of the physi'cian, and a resort to many expedients that only scientific knowledge could suggest, are necessary to expose the fraud.

I can offer only a suggestion or two on the subject. Careful attention ought to be given in the first place, in doubtful cases, to the manner in which, or the means by which the alleged injury is claimed to have been sustained; and will sometimes be sufficient to demonstrate that it could not have

been inflicted in that way; that the means were not adequate
to the end; or else, that if it had been produced in that way,
other and external consequences, plain to be seen, must have
accompanied it. I once saw a fictitious injury very clearly
exposed in court, by a medical expert. The case was one in
which injury to the vertebral nerves, resulting in partial par
alysis, was claimed to have been occasioned by the party hav
ing been pushed violently against the side of a door. The
physician had a living subject brought in, and undressed
before the jury, and proceeded to point out the situation and
protection of these nerves, and what sort of blow and by what
sort of an instrument would be necessary to reach them, with
out breaking through the protection in such manner as to
leave unmistakable and severe external injuries. No external
indications of violence were or had been apparent. And con
trasting the means by which it was alleged the nerves had been
wounded, with those that would be necessary to effect it without leaving visible exterior results, the physician was able to
demonstrate to the satisfaction of the jury, that the man could
not have been hurt in the way he claimed.

Critical examination may, also, in some of these cases, disclose that the injury complained of, even if actually sustained,
would not produce the resulting disease that is claimed to
exist.

A physician told me a very amusing instance of a case in
which he was summoned from a considerable distance, as a
witness, where a person had been assaulted by another, and
had commenced a suit for damages. Some medical gentle
men had examined him, and had decided that the claim he
set up was correct: that he had become paralyzed in his leg,
in consequence of an injury to certain nerves, sustained in the
affray. In the consultation they had in regard to the case,
these physicians pointed out what nerves were injured, and
how the result claimed had come to pass. "Why," gentlemen,
said the witness, "are you aware that the nerves you suppose

to be injured do not supply the leg?" No. they had not been aware of that. He sent for a chart of anatomy, and succeeded in making it plain to them, that injury to those nerves would not occasion paralysis of the leg, and the result was, the case went off, and I do not know what became of it afterwards. But, I said, " Doctor, how could you spoil so good a thing? Why did not you let them testify?" " Well," he replied, "they obtained their education at the school where I was professor of anatomy."

A third subject of inquiry in cases where deception is suspected, is the exact correspondence of the symptoms that are manifested, with those that belong to the disease which is claimed to exist. It is very difficult for an ordinary patient to counterfeit symptoms with sufficient accuracy to escape the detection of a thoroughly informed and closely observant physician, who has reason to be on his guard.

I remember a very interesting piece of testimony from a distinguished physician, in a railway accident case. The plaintiff came into court apparently suffering from partial paralysis, and very lame. He was obviously in a bad way altogether. The disease had even begun to invade the brain, and he had to have water poured on his head while he was testifying. The case looked promising for very serious damages. The physician who had been sent for as a witness, and had examined the party, testified before the jury that there was nothing whatever the matter with the man, and that he had not been hurt at all. This conclusion was quite in harmony with the circumstances of the accident, which was very slight, and not very likely to produce such serious results. Nor had the resulting disease made its appearance until a considerable time afterwards. But there had been an accident, and a railroad company was responsible, or would have been responsible if the plaintiff had been hurt. On cross examination the doctor was asked if the man was not very lame. " He certainly walked very lame," was the reply. "Could you discover any other cause for his lameness except the injury to which he attributed it ?" "No, sir, I could not." "Well, if he had sustained the injury that he said he had, would it not have produced lameness ?" "Most certainly." "Then, how are you enabled to state with so much confidence, that the man did not sustain the injury ?" "I will tell you," said the doctor: "he claimed to have paralysis of the muscles of the right thigh. Now if the muscles of the fore part of the thigh had been paralyzed, he would have walked in ths way, [illustrating it] ; the toes would have dropped first. If the paralysis had been behind, he would have walked thus, [illustrating]; the heel would have have dropped first ; and if it had involved the muscles on both sides of the limb, before and behind, the whole leg would have given way in the attempt to step, like this, [illustrating]. "Now," he continued, "this is the way the man was lame, [illustrating] which indicated only that one leg was shorter than the other. He did not claim that such was the case, and I measured his limbs and found it was not the case. It became certain, therefore, that he was not suffering from paralysis, and that his lameness was fictitious. And this was confirmed by the manner in which he walked when he thought no one was looking at him, when he showed no lameness at all."

Now if this rascal's physician, who had been drawn along by ingenious management into believing in this case, and into assisting to sustain it in court, had at the outset perceived that his patient was not too good to avail himself of an opportunity, and had borne in mind that he was dealing with a man capable of that sort of deception, he might have been led to test the case as he went along, when the patient was not aware that he was testing it ; and he might probably have arrived at a very different conclusion in regard to its character.

An excellent rule was stated to me by Dr. Holton, one of your professors, as having been adopted by him in cases of that sort. It was to require a patient to state to him with precision every symptom that he had, every pain or sensation, and exactly to locate it, and then carefully to write them down, just as stated by the patient, and at the time they were stated. In this way he was enabled at each successive interview, to preserve an unmistakable record of precisely what symptoms were from time to time claimed to exist, and to compare them with each other, as well as to preclude any dispute about the various statements made in regard to them. Such a course is very likely to detect spurious and inconsistent symptoms, and to prevent a party from changing his ground, as the emergency of his case might require.

He mentioned one case which he had occasion to examine, where, as the result of an accident, serious internal injury was claimed. The man complained of a severe pain in his kidneys, and of an affection of those organs consequent upon the hurt he had sustained. On being desired to point out the location of the pain, he placed it in a part of his back a good way from where the kidneys are usually found. On a subsequent visit, he still complained of the pain in those organs, and on being again requested to indicate the place, located it correctly; very naively remarking, "I have found out where the kidneys are situated, since you were here before."

Another very useful means of detection in these, as indeed, in all other cases of feigned disease or injury, is to watch the subject carefully, when he is not aware that he is seen. Few deceptions are so elaborately and perfectly carried out, as to be kept up while the patient is alone, and not exposed to observation, though even such instances have been known. Paralysis, lameness and deformity will often disappear when the mask is thrown off, which it might be very difficult to detect when the mask is on. Just as the manifestations of a fictitious insanity will subside, when there is no further occasion for their display.

But after all, as I have said before, the business of detective medicine, its means, its tests, its expedients, belong to medical

science and must be acquired by medical education. It is all
I can do, and all I seek to do, to draw your attention to the
importance of the subject, the frequency of its occurrence,
and the certainty of your being more or less concerned in it.
You must qualify yourselves by other instruction than mine,
to be equal to the requirements of the occasions that will
arise.

Of course you will not infer from what I have said in re
gard to these fictitious injuries, that there is not a very large
number of cases that are genuine, where to charge a decep
tion would be literally to add insult to injury. The majority
of mankind, let us be glad in believing, are not capable of de
ceptions of that sort. Their frequency is absolute, not relative.
The detective in medicine, as well as in police, is concerned
with the few, not with the many ; and the numerous meritorious
and genuine claims for judicial redress for such injuries, that
unhappily arise, should not be prejudiced by the prevalence of
fradulent claims of the same kind It is only necessary that
care should be taken, and sound, sagacious judgment employed,
in discriminating between the two ; and in trying to do that,
the physician like the lawyer, should become a judge of char
acter. The first and most important inquiry of all, is whether
the man is one from whom deception may be expected, when
opportunity offers, and temptation is strong. "The proper
study of mankind is man."

It is neither pleasant nor salutary to cultivate that sus
picious temper, that judges the motives and conduct of men
through glasses of the wrong color. The charitable and kind
ly spirit is far better. Nevertheless, in dealing with this
world, the fact must be recognized and remembered, that there
are those who are not beyond the reach of temptation, and
who when exposed to it will bear watching. To know how to
discriminate between this class and a better one, is a great
point to be gained, as well in the practice of medicine as
elsewhere.

LECTURE VIII.

RIGHTS AND LIABILITIES OF PHYSICIANS.

My subject, to-day, will be the rights and liabilities of physicians.

I remarked to you in a former lecture, that you have in most states of the Union, no monopoly of the practice of medicine or surgery. The tendency—unfortunately, as I think—of most legislation, has been to throw open the practice of the profession to whoever thinks proper to engage in it, and can obtain any patients to treat. In some of the states, however, the law still remains as it used to be almost everywhere, that either a license from a board constituted by the public authorities, or else a diploma from a recognized medical college, is necessary to entitle a physician to practice. I regret that such is not the law universally.

On the subject of the compensation of physicians for their services, the law can be stated in a very few words. The physician is entitled to, and can, if necessary, always maintain an action for, a reasonable compensation for his professional services; and what is a reasonable compensation, must be determined in view of all the circumstances, the nature of the engagement, the amount of time and attention bestowed, the responsibility and difficulty of the case. It is largely taken into consideration, also, in determining the amount, what have come to be the usual charges for similar services in the profession.

In England, where the learned professions are placed on
a somewhat different basis as to compensation, from that
which prevails in this country, the physician can maintain no
action for his fees. They are regarded as an *honorarium*
merely, and not as the subject of a legal contract. The fee is,
therefore, always paid to him when he makes the visit, and the
subject of money is never named between him and his patient.
He receives the usual fee quite as a matter of course, except
in special cases outside of the ordinary course of practice.

I will add one or two further suggestions in respect to
liability for physicians' fees, not always understood by gentlemen in your profession. Your legal claim is always against
the person who employs you. Yet, as is very often the case,
you may be called upon by some one other than the patient.
Whether you can hold that person for your compensation, in
cases where the patient is not a member of his family, depends
upon the question whether he employs the physician on his
own responsibility, or upon the responsibility of the patient.
In other words, with whom is the contract, as actually under
stood between the parties? And where the patient is not one for
whom the person calling in the physician is legally or morally
bound to provide, such person will not be liable for fees, unless
he, in some way assumes the responsibility, and so gives the
physician to understand: so that, as both parties understand,
the services are rendered, not on the credit of the patient, but
on that of the person by whom they were invited.

It sometimes occurs, also, that where attendance is given
upon the credit of the patient himself, some third person assumes to guarantee the responsibility of the patient, or agrees
to pay if the patient does not, or, in common phrase, to see
the physician paid. Such an undertaking is not legally bind
ing, unless expressed in writing. The distinction is between
the case in which the services are afforded on the original
responsibility of the person undertaking to pay, and are
charged to him in the first instance, and that in which the ser-

vices are charged to the patient, and the other person becomes collaterally bound that they shall be paid for. In the latter case, such contract must be in writing.

I need hardly add, that the right of a physician to main tain an action, does not extend to cases of attendance on a pa tient, however protracted, where the value of the services has been lost to the patient, through want of ordinary care and at tention, or of ordinary skill on the physician's part. In such case he has no right of action, and certainly ought to have none. The measure of recovery for services of any description, where no special agreement as to price exists, is what they are reason ably worth; and where by the fault of the party rendering them they are reasonably worth nothing, he has no legal claim.

This whole subject of professional compensation, in the medical as in all other professions, however, is to the high minded man, only a secondary consideration. It is an important one ; it is a very proper one. He that ministers at the altar, must live by the altar. It is due to yourselves—it is due to your profession—that justice should be done you in this par ticular. But it is after all a consideration that in the mind of a man who justly appreciates his profession, is far subordinate both to the calls of duty, and to the love he cherishes for his science and his art. A professional man, greedy of money, or who makes that the primary or principal object, will never attain eminence, and will usually fail to obtain even the money. All controversy and discussion on that subject, and lawsuits espec ially, should be avoided, unless in the extreme and rare case, where gross imposition upon the physician is attempted. The realizing of an adequate remuneration is rather a matter of tact and judicious attention, than one of law. Prompt and early settlements are not only for your own interest, but will be usually found agreeable to your patients. The good physician will rarely find any trouble on that score, where the patient has the ability ; and if he does, it is better generally to be rid

of the patient, and to pocket the loss, than to have any quarrel
about it.

I add one further practical suggestion on the subject of
fees, not as a matter of law, but drawn from my own observa
tion. It has seemed to me that your profession do not dis
criminate sufficiently in the matter of charges, between small
cases and great ones : between easy and ordinary services, and
those involving higher skill, greater responsibility, and more
serious consequences. I think it is too much their custom to
charge by the visit, without just distinction between the visit
to tell the patient there is nothing the matter with him, and
that which, perhaps, saves his life in a critical emergency.
This discrimination is made, I believe, in surgery, as it certainly
is in the legal profession ; and I see not why it should not be
extended to the general practice of medicine.

I pointed out to you in a former lecture, that the physi
cian is entitled to a reasonable compensation, when required to
attend as an expert witness. But as some inquiry has been
made on that point, I recur to it again. There is no doubt, in
the first place, that a physician may decline to obey a sub
pœna where it is made known to him that he is only required
to testify as an expert, and not to facts, and where proper
compensation is refused. That would undoubtedly be accepted by the court, as a reasonable excuse. The cases would be
rare, however, in which it would be judicious to take that
course : and it should very clearly appear that the physician is
summoned purely as an expert, and that compensation is dis
tinctly refused. But when the witness attends in obedience to
the subpœna, he may still decline to testify as an expert merely,
on the ground that proper compensation is refused him. Such
was the express decision of the court in England, in the case
of *Webb v. Page*, (1 *Carr. & Kir.* 23) ; and the right to
such compensation was also recognized by the same court, in
the case of *Willis v. Peckham*, (1 *Brod. & Bing.* 515). Be
sides, as I have before stated, irrespective of the question of

compensation, a witness may always decline to express opinions as an expert, if he pleases, and could thus protect his just rights in the premises, if there were no other way. Practically, however, this question will rarely be found attended with difficulty, as in proper cases suitable compensation is always paid, and will not be likely to be refused.

A physician is under no legal obligation to obey any call to attend a patient, and may always decline to do so. He may also cease his attendance at will, in any case where he has attended, provided he does not exercise this right so abruptly, or in such an emergency, that harm comes to the patient thereby; and a patient may at any time dismiss his physician at his own pleasure, whether he has paid him or not.

As to the liabilities of physicians, and first as to their liability criminally: there are various cases in which physicians may be criminally liable for their professional conduct.

First, there is in most states, a series of what may be called police or sanitary regulations, on the subject of the public health, registration, burials, etc., for a breach of which, physicians are liable to prosecution and fine. Of those it is only necessary to say, that all such provisions should receive the scrupulous observance of physicians, because they are generally wise regulations, and important to the public welfare. But if, in your judgment, they in any particular instance are not wise, and sometimes they are not, interest yourselves, if you please, in correcting them: such a movement comes very properly from your profession. But while they remain the law, observe them; set the example of always obeying the law of the land, scrupulously; if it is wrong, get it amended, if you can. It is a bad example, and a pernicious one, for gentlemen of a learned profession to set to humbler classes in society, ever to permit yourselves to disregard any statute law, however useless or unwise it may seem to be.

A physician may be made liable for manslaughter in his treatment of a case. It is to be regretted, in my judgment, that this principle of the law is not more generally understood, and more frequently enforced; I do not mean against regular physicians—I have never seen any case of that kind, or heard of one,—but against those who take advantage of the liberality of the law that I have referred to, to practice medicine without adequate qualification. There is a limit to the right of a man to deal with and experiment upon human life, even when he does not mean to destroy it.

A person may be liable for manslaughter by treating a patient, when death ensues from the treatment, in three cases: In the first place, where he is guilty of gross ignorance; where he attempts to deal medically or surgically with a case, in respect to the important elements of which he is grossly igno rant. It is not very easy, in words, to explain the distinction between what may be called ignorance, and gross ignorance. By gross ignorance is meant, as well as I can state it, extreme ignorance, that amounts to recklessness. It may perhaps be defined in this way: where the party is not only ignorant, but knows that he is ignorant. If I were to undertake, for instance, to amputate a limb; I am not sufficiently acquainted with the position of the arteries, and the manner of dealing with them, to do it with any reasonable prospect of success. I know that I am not sufficiently acquainted. It is not a mis take of judgment on my part, in a matter where I have reason to suppose I am properly informed: I know that I am not sufficiently instructed to be able to cut off a man's leg. The patient bleeds to death, simply from my want of the requisite knowledge; that is manslaughter, whatever efforts I may have made to save his life. On the other hand, having been fairly instructed in legal science, I might suppose that I had a correct view of a doubtful question of law, and have some rea sonable ground to think so. It turns out I am entirely mis taken, and a better lawyer might perceive that I was plainly mistaken; that, whatever mischief might come of it, and though it might be ignorance, would not be gross ignorance of the law; while it would be a mistake—perhaps an unfortunate mistake—it would not be one which I should be legally liable for the consequences of. In that case, I did not know that I was ignorant. I thought and had reason to suppose, that I understood the point correctly. In the other case that I supposed, I know, to start with, that I am uninstructed, and that I ought not to touch a matter of that sort, that may involve human life.

I need not dwell upon this subject. The rule of law founded on it, applies principally to quacks and impostors. It will have no application to any gentleman who proposes to graduate from an institution like this, or from any respectable medical college, before entering upon practice, because gross ignorance can not be predicated of a mind as well informed as yours must be, to obtain a diploma in the regular way.

There have been cases—I should say in stating the law on the subject of manslaughter, as I have done—there have been cases in which it has been held, that a person was not liable for a death occasioned by medical treatment, if the treatment was in good faith, however ignorant the practitioner. That if I were to undertake, without medical education, to prescribe for a sick man, and should administer to him a teaspoonful of arsenic, and he should die, it would be justifiable, legally, because I did not want, nor intend to kill him, but desired to cure him; and really I did not know that arsenic is a poison, or that a teaspoonful is a sufficient dose to destroy life. I have only to say that I am very sorry, and will try and remember not to do it again. That is not the law, as established by the best and highest authorities; it is not the law that is consistent with reason and justice. To destroy human life by attempting to tamper with it, when grossly and consciously ignorant of the disease and the remedy, is manslaughter in the eye of the law.

Then a physician may be liable for manslaughter in the treatment of a patient, though sufficiently informed, where he is guilty of gross negligence. He knows enough to have avoided the fatal treatment, but he is grossly negligent in the care of the case. As I said just now, in respect to gross ignorance, it is not very easy to define in language, even to lawyers, the various legal degrees of negligence, slight, ordi nary and gross. It is a subject which has been very much discussed, and it is difficult to state with precision, the distinction between what is called the want of ordinary care, which I shall have occasion to allude to presently, as the foundation for a civil action, and gross negligence, which ren ders the party liable criminally. I can only say that the latter is that neglect that is plain, obvious, and indefensible; the sort of neglect that no one would attempt to justify, or to esteem as any degree of care. A man may prescribe when he is drunk, and in several states—quite unnecessarily—that is made, by special statute, manslaughter, if death ensues from it. If a prescription is given in a state of intoxication by a physician, and it occasions death, it would be manslaughter, without any such statute. So, gross carelessness in writing a prescription, in writing down one thing when you meant to have written down another, and what you have written is poisonous, and death ensues, that is gross negligence. So, if you were writing a prescription, and you put down a large quantity when you intended a small one, and in the large quantity the substance is a fatal poison, and you kill the pa tient. So, if in dealing out medicines by one who is dispensing them, by mere carelessness he gives the poisonous one instead, of the beneficial, or the plainly fatal quantity instead of the curative one, and death is caused. Because the degree of care must be proportioned to the importance of the occasion; and negligence that in a small matter might not be regarded as gross, becomes so when it involves human life.

These are but illustrations. Of course ordinary mistakes, errors in judgment, errors in treatment, in diagnosis, in skill, which few physicians are so fortunate as to go through life without making, do not constitute gross negligence. Sometimes the result may be very unfortunate. You may actually kill your patient, by an error in judgment as to what is the matter with him, or as to the remedy that ought to be applied. But the law, in its criminal application, takes a merciful view of human error, in that respect, as long as you bring to bear even a very moderate measure of skill and care; I mean so long as you are not guilty of gross ignorance, or gross, indefensible negligence. You may destroy your unhappy patients until you entitle yourself to such an epitaph as was once inscribed on the tombstone of a physician in a country church yard: "*Si monumentum quæris, circumspice!*" "If you seek my monument, behold the graves by which I am surrounded!" You may do all that, without being liable criminally. Negligence such as entails that consequence—gross negligence, is such as evinces a wanton disregard for human life. On the same principle that an engineer of a train is held guilty of manslaughter, for destroying the lives of the passengers by running without looking at the signals which would show him that the switch was wrong, or by recklessly running on the known time of another train, liable to be encountered.

There is a third way in which physicians may be guilty, in the treatment of patients, of the crime of manslaughter, and that is by performing operations to produce abortion, or miscarriage, upon a woman; because such operations are expressly forbidden by law, and are made felonious—that is to say, state's prison offences, even when death does not ensue. If death does ensue from such an operation prohibited by law, that is manslaughter, and a high degree of manslaughter; much higher than those cases which arise under the circumstances I have tried to point out, by means of gross negligence, or gross ignorance. In those, there is at least the absence of a positive intent to commit crime. But where the act engaged in is in itself criminal, whatever the result may

be, if it happens to occasion death, the offence is little short
of murder.

As I have said, even if death does not ensue, such an
operation is a state's prison offence, and always ought to be:
this destruction of unborn life. And the attention of physi
cians cannot be too earnestly called to the great importance of
the observance of the statute on that subject, whatever the
temptation, and whatever the importunity. It is a law that it
is doubly unsafe to disregard, because public opinion backs
it up, as you are aware, with great force, and it is punished
with great severity. And it is a wise and humane law, that
never ought to be disregarded, even if it could be done with
impunity. I except, of course, from these remarks, those
cases where such operations becom necessary to save life.

Coming now to the subject of the civil liability of phy
sicians for their profe sional conduct, that is to say, their lia
bility to respond in damages to those who have suffered by
it, we reach one of the most troublesome pieces of business a
practitioner of medicine is ever likely to be involved in : actions for malpractice, as they are commonly called. It is easy
enough for a competent and careful physician to escape any
such legal liability : to escape, I mean, making himself right-
fully amenable to an action of that sort. But it is by no
means easy, always, to escape from unjust and unfounded
claims of that character. The rule of law that regulates that
liability, is very simple. And you will readily perceive when
it is stated, that no man who assumes to practice as a physician, and who thus invites the confidence of many who are not
able to judge of his qualifications, if he cannot, or does not
come up to that requirement, is entitled to much sympathy.
The rule is this: the physician or surgeon must bring to the
discharge of his professional duty, ordinary skill, and ordinary
care. If he does that, he is not legally responsible for the

result, be it what it may, even though it could be plainly shown that it arose from his mistake or defective judgment. Ordinary skill cannot be better defined, so far as I know, than to say it is what would be regarded as the average skill of the average physician. It is not a high requirement; no man who respects himself, or has any love for his profession, would ever care to rest satisfied with the attainment of only ordinary skill. Preliminary education, which you have to get through with before you commence the practice of your profession, is one thing; the real education goes on afterwards as long as you live. But the requirement of the law is moderate, and ordinary skill is all that you are legally compelled to bring to the service of your patients: the ordinary skill of the ordinary physician. Is the treatment in question such as the generality of common physicians would approve? If it is, however mistaken in its application to that particular case, however plain it may be that you might have done better, there is no legal responsibility, medically or surgically.

The same rule defines the degree of care: it is ordinary care: not the best care, not unusual care, or desirable care, or the care that often saves life in doubtful cases; common care, such as the common average of physicians would use; such, at least, as the pauper in the poor-house receives from the hireling, to whom his life or death is a matter of no consequence. So much and no more, the law demands.

Claims of malpractice are usually made in surgical cases; not because they could not as well be predicated upon medical malpractice, but because it is so difficult to trace the consequences of erroneous treatment in the medical case, where, with the best of treatment, the patient will often die, and with the worst of treatment he will sometimes happily recover: it is so difficult to trace the cause and effect, and to be able to show, by legal evidence, that the death of the person, or his ill health was a consequence of the treatment, except in the rare cases where some great impropriety of treatment has occurred, that it is not often attempted. I have known such cases, but they are very rare. These claims ordinarily occur in surgery, where a man fails to recover entirely from an injury which has been surgically treated, and remains more or less a cripple, or deformed, afterwards. Those are usually the cases in which actions for malpractice arise.

As you all know, there is a certain class of cases, inju ries, fractures, dislocations, etc., where the patient may obtain a perfect cure, and he may not. It may depend upon the constitution, habits, or age of the patient, it may depend upon the daily care he receives, it may depend upon various circumstances, and of course it depends very much upon the treatment. In some such case the patient fails to get well; he has had a hard time of it; it is easy for him to think that the physician has not done right, that he might have done better, that if he had been dealing with a rich and influential party whose business he was anxious to obtain, he would have been more careful. Perhaps the patient finds some other physician, who tells him the course pursued was not the best. It is so much easier to point out an error afterwards, than to an ticipate it. Such are the cases that arise, and unfortunately for the profession, they have to be determined by juries, who are the most incompetent judges possible, of such questions. I hope to see the time when all cases of personal inju ry, or alleged personal injury, made the foundation of actions for damages, will be referred by the court, at the instance of either party to the cause, to a competent body of medical experts, disinterested and disconnected with the case, who shall have power to hear the parties, and the story of the attending physicians, to call to their aid any medical evidence they may think desirable, to examine the patient as much as they please, to take their own time, and finally to determine whether the man is hurt, how much he is hurt, whether he is likely to get well, and when, and all that can be determined by medical skill. And so in case of malpractice, if the injury remain, to determine whether or not it is the result of mistreatment on the part of the physician, through the want of ordinary skill or ordinary care; and then let that fact so settled enter into the record, and form the basis of such damages as the proper tribunal may award, in case the liability of the party is made out. But as the law stands at present, a man commences an action for malpractice against his physician, brings him before a jury, and upon such medical evidence as can be had upon one side and the other, often conflicting, the jury come to a conclusion which is a good deal more likely to be wrong than right. But the legal test on which turns the question whether the physician ought to be charged or not, depends, after all, upon the rule of law that I have stated, did he exercise in the business, ordinary care, and ordinary skill.

One further suggestion. Even if the physician is wanting in ordinary care or ordinary skill, if the resulting injury is in any part the consequence of the negligence of the party himself, in that case he is not entitled to recover. The law does not measure the proportion of mutual misconduct; if the result is the fault of both sides, if the surgeon has mistreated the case, and the patient by his carelessness, negligence, or improper conduct has contributed to the result, that exonerates the physician from legal liability.

Malpractice cases against physicians are very much like epidemic diseases; when they are prevalent in a community, then it is necessary to look out for them. It is curious, but it is nevertheless true, how such things are propagated through newspaper and telegraphic reports; just as suicides—suicides in a certain way, perhaps a very strange way—will get started, and run through the country like an epidemic. Particular forms of murder or assassination run in the same way, like the case of a man's murdering a woman because she will not marry him, and then killing himself. Some poor wretch commits such an act, it is published everywhere, and the conta-

13

gion of it spreads all over the country. So with certain actions at law, not of very common occurrence, when they get started, they will have a run until checked by repeated defeat. Quite a number of years ago, there was an epidemic of malpractice cases in this state. A considerable number of them were pending at the same time. They were all, so far as I know, with out just foundation, and it is creditable to the courts, that they were all ultimately defeated. There was some temporary success, but the final result was in favor of the physicians. That quelled the epidemic. Since then, so far as I am in formed, there has not been such a cause in the state.

Physicians should be very careful how they encourage such claims against other physicians, by their opinion or their evidence. Of course, when a case of actual malpractice arises, when a party has a legal right to redress against a physician, and your evidence is called for, you have to state the truth. But physicians should be very careful how they encourage such actions by their opinion or their testimony, until they are very clear that the claims are well founded. It is not enough to be clear that the physician was wrong, not enough to be clear, even, that some permanent injury was the fault of the physician; but you should be clear that he was so far wrong, that he can be legally and properly convicted of the want either of ordinary care, or of ordinary skill. Aside from the injustice done, it is a poor and shabby way of striking a blow at a rival, from which an honorable man would shrink. And curses of that kind generally come home to roost.

One or two practical suggestions, in conclusion, that may be useful to you in keeping clear of this unfortunate class of litigation. In dealing with doubtful surgical cases, and with people of doubtful character, where that sort of man is afflicted with that sort of an injury, leave him, if you can, to be treated by a more courageous surgeon. But if you are compelled to treat such a case, and in which a perfect cure may be doubtful, after you have done your best, make that plain at the starting point, to the man and his friends. Let them understand that the result is going, in your estimation, to be doubtful. If they prefer to avail themselves of the skill of some more confident man, let them relieve you; but if not, let your prognosis be distinctly understood in the outset. Do not leave it in their power to turn about in the end, and to charge you with having promised a cure, or a satisfactory result· Place it the other way, so that you will be able to say, and to prove, if the end is unfortunate, that you never have promised any thing different, and that the result has only verified your expressed fears.

Then if you are treating such a case, and dealing with per sons not incapable of prosecuting you afterwards, unjustly, avail yourself, as you go along, of the best medical counsel and assistance. Do not stand alone. So that if you should ever be called upon in such a suit, it will not appear that you have assumed the whole responsibility, but on the other hand, that you have brought to your aid the best assistance that was available. And you have the very important benefit of the evidence of such an associate; not merely the evidence of his subsequent opinion, but of an opinion formed during the progress of the case, and in respect to the treatment that had his sanction, and was conducted under his advice.

Yet, if, in spite of all precautions, you still get involved in a controversy of that sort, where you are on the right side of it, and where it becomes your duty to yourself and your profession to vindicate your conduct, I can only advise you in that event, to engage wise and judicious counsel, put him fully in possession of all the facts of the case, follow his instructions, and above all things hold your tongue. Parties do themselves great injury, sometimes, by talking about their cases; forgetting that what they say is evidence against them, and is very likely to be misrepresented or misunderstood.

Litigation is always more or less uncertain, especially when it depends on the verdicts of juries. Physicians have

been made liable unjustly, sometimes, in spite of all exertions
in their behalf.   They have, perhaps, sometimes, though more
rarely, been acquitted when they ought to have been made
liable.   It is not necessarily an imputation upon a physician
to be defeated in such an action; nor is it always a justifica
tion to obtain a verdict in his favor.

This concludes what I am able to say to you, on the sub
ject of medical jurisprudence.   Of course you will not infer,
that I have by any means covered the whole ground, in these
very few lectures.   Many topics I have been compelled to omit
altogether, and those I have dealt with, I have had no time
to discuss thoroughly or completely.   I have tried to be plain
and useful, rather than learned or philosophical.   And I have
accomplished all that I attempted, if I have succeeded in fur
nishing you with such practical suggestions on the various
points, as you may be able to remember, and to make serviceable in your future professional life.

UNIVERSITY OF VERMONT,

MEDICAL DEPARTMENT.

BURLINGTON, VERMONT.

TWENTY-NINTH SESSION. 1882.

FACULTY OF MEDICINE.

MATTHEW HENRY BUCKHAM, A. M., D. D., Burlington. Vt., President.

SAMUEL WHITE THAYER, M. D., LL. D.. Burlington, Vt., Emeritus Professor of General and Special Anatomy, Professor of Hygiene and State Medicine, consulting Surgeon to Mary Fletcher Hospital.

*****WALTER CARPENTER, M. D.,** Burlington, Vt., Professor of Theory and Practice of Medicine, consulting Physician to Mary Fletcher Hospital.

JOHN ORDRONAUX, M. D., LL. D., New York City, Emeritus Professor of Medical Jurisprudence.

A. F. A. KING, M. D., Washington, D. C., Professor of Obstetrics and the Diseases of Women, consulting Physician to Mary Fletcher Hospital.

WILLIAM DARLING, A. M., F. R. C. S., LL. D., New York City, Professor of General and Special Anatomy.

HENRY D. HOLTON, A. M., M. D., Brattleboro, Vt., Professor of Materia Medica and General Pathology, consulting Surgeon to Mary Fletcher Hospital.

JAMES L. LITTLE, M. D., New York City, Professor of the Principles and Practice of Surgery, consulting Surgeon to Mary Fletcher Hospital,

A. P. GRINNELL, M.D., Burlington, Vt., Professor of Physiology and Microscopic Anatomy, attending Physician to Mary Fletcher Hospital.

RUDOLPH A. WITTHAUS, A. M., M. D., New York City, Professor of Chemistry and Toxicology.

PROFESSORS OF SPECIAL SUBJECTS.

ROBERT W. TAYLOR, M. D., New York City, Professor of Diseases of the Skin.

A. T. WOODWARD, M. D., Brandon, Vt., Professor of the Surgical Diseases of Women, consulting Physician to Mary Fletcher Hospital.

D. B. ST. JOHN ROOSA, A. M., M. D., New York City, Professor of the Diseases of the Eye and Ear.

*The resignation of Professor CARPENTER, which takes effect at the end of the present session, will create a vacancy in this Chair, which will be filled at the next annual meeting in June, 1881.

STEPHEN M. ROBERTS, A. M., **M. D.**, New York City, Professor of Diseases of Children.

GEORGE M. GARLAND, A. M., **M. D.**, Boston, Mass., Professor of Thoracic Diseases.

WM. J. MORTON, A. M., **M. D.**, New York City, Professor of the Diseases of the Mind and Nervous System.

CLINTON WAGNER, **M. D.**, New York City, Professor of Diseases of the Throat.

SAMUEL WHITE THAYER, **M. D.**, **LL. D.**, Professor of Hygiene and State Medicine.

EDWARD J. PHELPS, Esq., Professor of Medical Jurisprudence. Demonstrator of Anatomy.

HOSPITAL ADVANTAGE.—The Mary Fletcher Hospital, with its commodious ampitheatre, is open for clinical instruction during the session. The Medical and Surgical Clinics of the College will be held in the amphitheatre attached to the Hospital. In addition to these regular clinics of the College, Instructions will be given at the bedside by the Professors of the Medical Department of the University.

LECTURES ON SPECIAL SUBJECTS.—These Lectures by gentlemen well known as authorities, recognized in their particular departments, will be delivered during the regular session, without extra expense.

CLINICS.—Besides these Lectures, there will be Clinics held as follows: SURGICAL CLINIC, by Professor LITTLE, every Saturday from 9 to 12, during the last half of the session.

MEDICAL CLINIC, by Professor CARPENTER or Professor GRINNELL, on Wednesday morning during the first half of the term, and by Professor KING during the last half of the term.

CLINIC FOR DISEASES OF NERVOUS SYSTEM, by Professor MORTON, during his course.

CLINIC FOR DISEASES OF EYE AND EAR, by Professor ROOSA, during his course of Lectures.

CLINIC FOR DISEASES OF SKIN, by Professor TAYLOR, during his course.

CLINIC FOR DISEASES OF CHILDREN, by Professor ROBERTS.

CLINIC FOR DISEASES OF THROAT, by Professor CLINTON WAGNER.

CLINIC FOR THORACIC DISEASES, by Professor GEORGE M. GARLAND,

THE PRELIMINARY TERM, consisting of a course of Lectures and Recitations in the various branches of Medicine and Surgery, will begin on the FIRST THURSDAY OF NOVEMBER, 1881, and continue until MARCH 1ST, 1882. Fee, $30.

THE REGULAR WINTER SESSION will commence on the FIRST THURSDAY OF MARCH, 1882, and continue SIXTEEN WEEKS. This course will consist of from five to six Lectures daily in the various departments of Medicine and Surgery.

FEES FOR THE REGULAR SESSION:

MATRICULATION FEE, payable each term, - - $ 5 00
FEES for the full course of Lectures by all the Professors, 70 00
GRADUATION FEE, - - - - - - 25 00

Material for dissection will be furnished at cost. The tickets are to be taken out at the beginning of the session.

Students who have already attended two full courses of Lectures in other regular Schools are admitted on paying the matriculation fee and $25. Students who have attended two full courses in this College, or who having attended one full course in some regularly established Medical School, and one full course in this College, are admitted to a third course of Lectures on paying the matriculation fee only. GRADUATES of this School are admitted without fee. GRADUATES of other REGULAR SCHOOLS and THEOLOGICAL STUDENTS are admitted on general ticket by paying the matriculation fee. Good board can be obtained at reasonable rates.

For further particulars and Circulars apply to the Secretary,

Prof. A. P. GRINNELL, M. D.,

BURLINGTON.

www.ingramcontent.com/pod-product-compliance
Lightning Source LLC
Chambersburg PA
CBHW030550270326
41927CB00008B/1587